See Me Naked

See Me Naked

Stories of Sexual Exile in American Christianity

Amy Frykholm

Beacon Press, Boston

Beacon Press
25 Beacon Street
Boston, Massachusetts 02108-2892
www.beacon.org

Beacon Press books
are published under the auspices of
the Unitarian Universalist Association of Congregations.

14 13 12 11   8 7 6 5 4 3 2 1

This book is printed on acid-free paper that meets the uncoated paper
ANSI/NISO specifications for permanence as revised in 1992.

Text design and composition by Wilsted & Taylor Publishing Services

Many names and identifying characteristics of people mentioned in this
work have been changed to protect their identities.

Library of Congress Cataloging-in-Publication Data
Frykholm, Amy Johnson.
See me naked : stories of sexual exile in American Christianity /
by Amy Frykholm.
p. cm.
ISBN 978-0-8070-0466-1 (hardcover : alk. paper)
1. Sex—Religious aspects—Protestant churches. 2. Protestants—
United States—Sexual behavior. I. Title.
BR517.F79 2011
261.8'35709730905 1—dc22   2011012340

To St. George Mission, Leadville,
for your ongoing, healing work

Contents

Introduction: Exile

In the fall of 2006, just before the midterm elections, Ted Haggard—celebrated pastor of the fourteen-thousand-member New Life Church in Colorado Springs, spiritual counselor to President George W. Bush, president of the National Association of Evangelicals—was suspended from his position in light of a scandal involving sex and drugs.

Michael Forest Jones, an escort and masseur in Denver, Colorado, alleged that he had carried on a three-year sexual relationship with Haggard in which the famous pastor had paid him for sex and to procure methamphetamines. After his resignation, Haggard wrote to his congregation, "There is a part of my life that is so repulsive and dark that I've been warring against it all of my adult life."

Haggard never says that this "part" is his sexuality, in particular homosexual desire, but perhaps that is obvious. He has been at war with an intimate and elemental part of himself that he had tried to send into permanent exile, without success. In the light of day, he was a model husband and father of four children. Every Sunday, his blonde and photogenic wife, Gayle, dutifully played her role in the front row of the cavernous New Life auditorium. Haggard often gestured toward their family life, and Gayle publicly worried that people in the church thought their marriage was "so perfect." But by night, in the "darkness," Haggard was driven by desires that seemed beyond his control. "From time to time," he wrote, "the dirt I thought was gone would resurface, and I would find myself thinking thoughts and experiencing desires that were contrary to everything I believe and teach."

I watched Haggard's fall from grace with fascination. I was deep into the research for this book, and on the day that Haggard's story broke, I was interviewing one participant about the relationship between spirituality and sexuality at a diner in Boulder, Colorado, looking out onto the sidewalk at newspaper headlines about Haggard. A year before, I had been part of a History Channel production that was partially filmed at New Life Church. I had spent several odd minutes in Haggard's office when he was not present, watching the fish swim around in his fish tank and looking at the titles of the books on his shelves. And in fact, when this documentary aired in the summer of 2006, Michael Forest Jones saw it and for the first time recognized his client, whom he had known by the name of "Art."

As I was researching this book, I identified New Life as a microcosm of American religion with its strange blend of marketing, charismatic personalities, "Bible-based" teaching, and latte bars. So I had started spending time there, attending occasional worship services, and observing the social dynamics of the place. Both before and after Haggard's demise, I'd sensed an erotic energy that intrigued me. Certainly it wasn't overt, and I am expecting that readers may laugh at me when I mention it. But my sense is, on the level of instinct, that people are drawn to New Life Church in part because of a potent sexual energy. They project their desires onto the shaggy-haired men with guitars onstage. They feel caught up in the enlivening energy of being a part of something larger than themselves— something more spectacular and more beautiful than themselves. When Gayle and Ted occupied their places front and center, members of the congregation projected their own fantasies and hopes about heterosexual marriage onto the handsome couple and idolized their intimacy. When I was in Ted Haggard's office, waiting my turn in front of the filming crew's cameras, his nervous young assistant stroked my hair and said, "This is what I do for Pastor Ted before he goes on camera."

I think, however, I am also fascinated by Ted Haggard's situation because I recognize his dilemma, specifically his desire to keep his spirituality and his sexuality locked up in different boxes, in terror of what would happen if the two were to come together in the public eye. Not only do I recognize this dilemma in myself, but I also saw and heard about it from many of the people that I interviewed for this book. Spirituality and sexuality, for many people in American society and perhaps especially Christians, are kept rigidly separate, and many struggle to find a way to reconcile the religious elements of their lives and their sexual realities.

On the one hand, we can look at this dilemma culturally and recognize that we come by it naturally. In a body-obsessed yet body-hating culture, where sex is for sale twenty-four hours a day, perhaps it is a relief to check our bodies at the door when we go to church. American Christianity has taught that the only viable relationship between body and spirit is a proper following of the rules. "God's plan" for human sexuality is a familiar theme in churches, and while this "plan" may or may not line up with our experiences, we judge ourselves by it. American Christianity promises a life lived happily ever after to anyone who waits for sex until marriage, marries a religious person, and raises children in the church. The fact that this scenario describes fewer and fewer of us with each passing day is of little account.

The problem, however, is that "the rules" as they are taught to us and presented as an alternative to an out-of-control culture of sexual obsession actually serve to make the problem worse. They underscore a fundamental divide between the body and the spirit, and they deprive us of one of the key insights of Christianity: that the body is a vehicle of the holy, that its experiences in the world are a means of divine communication, and the body, with all its struggles, pains, and difficulties, can lead us into a more full relationship with God. And not only when we follow the rules and do everything right—even when life is complicated, beautiful, and strange, as life nearly always is.

As I interviewed people, I sought to understand the relationship between bodies and spirits, between sexuality and spirituality, on both personal and cultural levels. Specifically, I sought ways that sexuality and spirituality could come together, could live in harmony, where the body with all its tenacious strangeness could come home from exile. Each story told here emerges out of a unique set of circumstances, but unites with others to offer a picture of the relationship between spirituality and sexuality in one segment of American society. I focused on the stories of Protestant Christians because the problem I am trying to diagnose has significant Protestant roots. While Catholic stories might have similarities with those told here, they will also have differences, and those differences should not be papered over.

The people in this book, while they come from many different geographic and religious corners, share one culture. They share the pain of a toxic culture of religion and sexuality. Themes of shame, isolation, fear, silence, and vulnerability surface and resurface. At the same time, the healing and wholeness that many have found is also part of the same fabric. When one person works toward healing, we all step closer to it. If we see that we share this religious space, we might start using our stories, our bodies, our sexualities, our minds, and our souls to love one another better.

The stories that I tell here are not "mine," but I am the one who heard them and turned them into the form that you find here. While I did my best to give participants a chance to interact with their stories, they remain my interpretation of someone else's story. As in a game of telephone, I am certain that I say things here in a way that participants did not quite say them. In addition, in order to protect the identities of those who graciously offered their stories, I intentionally changed details, which inevitably changed meanings as well. In other words, each story is a collaboration, a meeting place, a conversation. It is not a perfect rendition of another person's reality.

Occasionally, participants chose a language for their experiences that is intensely graphic and might be offensive to some readers. In certain cases, I decided to leave this language alone and not transform it into something nice and easy to hear. When someone has the courage to find words for his or her experience, even when these words are painful, graphic, and even violent, I want to respect that language and the struggle from which it came. These are not fables, and they are not compilations. These stories are messy. They do not come together neatly in the end with a moral and a clear sense of direction. Each story has a number of interpretations, and the decisions that each person makes could be debated. One interviewee said to me, "Be sure you tell people that I am still not sure I made the right choices." That ongoing inner struggle is an important part of each of these stories and of our own. But through stories, we can begin to make sense of where we come from and where we are going. Genevieve, whose story is told in the third section of this book, noted the significance that storytelling, in itself, has had in her own experience. "People who told their stories started getting better," she said. "The people who kept their stories to themselves didn't."

A story, writes Barbara Brown Taylor, "creates a quiet place where one may lay down one's defenses for a while. A story does not ask for a decision. Instead, it asks for identification, which is how transformation begins." That is the hope embedded in this book: that as we cross into the realm of other people's stories, we might begin our own transformations, we might begin to live more fully and more completely as both spiritual and sexual beings. My hope is that these stories will open up your story and my story, and that telling will change us.

Part One

Wilderness

I sat on the floor in my bedroom on the far side of my desk where I could imagine it as a shield. My desk was the place where I kept the candy-scented erasers that my girlfriends and I bought at the mall, where I kept my notebooks full of pencil-written stories, and my diaries where I recorded my secrets. Yet no diary or notebook was private enough for the work I was engaged in at this moment. I had in my hand a small stenographer's notebook that I had taken from next to the phone downstairs. Next to me was the garbage can. My plan was to write what I needed to write and then tear the paper into tiny pieces and throw it away.

On one side of the paper, I wrote "OK." On the other, I wrote, "Not OK." I was fifteen and in the spring of my sophomore year of high school. This crisis had been precipitated by my new boyfriend. Out of his ash-smelling family room, I would emerge several hours after school had ended—flushed, frightened, elated, the holder of a new privacy. He touched and kissed me until I was literally faint with guilt and desire. He was chaos without boundaries, a terrifying ocean. I was desperately trying to get my bearings and draw myself a map out of the wilderness.

Not OK: I knew certain things were not OK. Intercourse, for example. I had no intention of going that far. That seemed like almost too firm a boundary to write down. Writing things down, I discovered as I sat there with a pencil, had a way of making things less firm. It had the opposite effect than the one I wanted. By naming what was "Not OK" I was acknowledging that such actions existed and that they were optional enough to need categorizing. The ground felt shaky.

OK: Kissing. That was easy.

But what about the touching of me that felt so wonderful? What about the games of desire that he played, communicating his brown-eyed want of me that far exceeded my squeamishness about particular acts, that seemed to outweigh my will? I didn't even have words for that. I couldn't fit it in my columns.

Sitting there with the failure of my experiment, I didn't feel that I had anyone to talk to. My parents would be, perhaps justifiably, horrified. I had only one friend at the time, a girl from my church youth group who had such sunny innocence that I didn't want to sully her with what I imagined to be my darkness. I felt very much alone, stranded, and helpless.

As planned, I destroyed the evidence of my inner negotiation, but I didn't succeed in changing anything. My relationship with this boy lasted only a few months. It could only briefly endure parental disapproval, my own private terror, and his carelessness, but it was enough to have married us off to each other in a previous century. And it shadowed my entire adolescence. I sensed that sexuality was dangerous, secret, and dark. It was a wilderness into which I felt I had been drawn against my will. Despite my attempts to draw myself a map, I remained unable to navigate.

Eventually, through my Baptist church youth group, I received a map. The map came in the form of workbooks written by a man named Dawson McAllister, and the rules were, at least on the surface, very clear: all touching and kissing leads to sex. Sex is something sinful until marriage. Therefore, touching and kissing are to be avoided. Church appeared as a fortress in the wilderness where I could take shelter. My youth group went to Dawson McAllister's rallies and workshops and accepted his version as God's own truth. Even so, my earlier taste of sexuality's chaos meant that I couldn't quite orient myself to this map. I believed that it was right, an accurate course to chart, but I couldn't quite apply it.

At the same time that I was learning about sex, I was also finding a similar dynamic with food. I went on my first diet in the fifth grade, a habit that continued long into adulthood. I was constantly in search of the right way to eat. All around me was indulgent food, and one of the most indulgent places was the church potluck. The tables groaned with chicken in cream sauce, chocolate chip bars, coconut pudding, and a thousand other Midwest culinary delights. In the midst of all that abundance, I existed on Diet Coke, tuna fish, and unbuttered whole-wheat toast. At the height of my participation in these bacchanal feasts, my weight dropped to eighty-five pounds.

Two things became related in my mind: taste and touch. If I could restrain the pleasure of each, I could choose to do what was right. I would not fall into the two great sins of my culture: obesity and promiscuity. It was all or nothing; Heaven or Hell. But seeping in around the edges were tastes of an extraordinary world of the senses. There were the French fries with ketchup and mayonnaise that I could pick up from the drive-through on my way home from school. There were the greasy packages of Potato Olés that I sopped in taco sauce late at night at Taco

John's. There were my boyfriend's touches in secret places. In the midst of my studious restraint, the possibility that any food or any touch could pitch me into the chasm of desire was real to me. Indulgence and guilt; repentance and practiced restraint. I was good at the dynamic. Eventually I trained myself not to taste or to feel, so as not to get caught unaware in the midst of passion.

But if I did fail, I could make a secret confession to my secret God who could then mete out secret punishment. I could simultaneously sin through indulgence and punish myself for sin by not tasting or feeling. My inner self kept a little bag packed at all times, so that she could hitch a ride to the far corners of my consciousness whenever delicious food or delicious touch was available. Thus, I developed a habit of self-alienation. While my particular method might be unique to me, I don't think the sense of self-estrangement and the perception that the world is full of dangerous pleasures are unique to me. These are a significant part of the American Christian culture in which I was raised. I was trained to police the boundaries of pleasure so as not to be drawn too deeply into the wilderness.

Years later, as I was trying to undo some of these trenchant dynamics, to come home to myself, I was on a long solitary road trip through Iowa. Late at night, I was flipping channels on the car radio when I heard a familiar voice. I stopped scanning. The voice was Dawson McAllister. He was conducting a call-in radio show for teens on a Christian radio station on the same subject for which I had often turned to him for advice: sex.

I listened as the calls came in, teen after teen, in the midst of the wilderness, calling out as I had done. They described to Dawson the darkness of their lives—the pregnant teenage girl, the sexually abused boy, the suicidal boy whose girlfriend had just rejected him, the girl whose mother was selling sex out of her house. When Dawson's clear iteration of "God's plan" failed them, one after another, he referred the caller to his "prayer line," where he said there was someone waiting who could pray with the teen. In these thickets of pain, Dawson McAllister's clarity and certainty seemed of little use.

As the lights flashed outside my window and I finally turned the radio off, I was struck by how messy and inconclusive life is and what a poor hand is dealt to young people in our culture. Part of Dawson McAllister's work, at least in my life, was to maintain the illusion of absolutes, of clear and impassable lines. He wanted to convince us that life, if we let it, could be contained by just a few biblical principles, properly applied. He had communicated this to me in his raspy, even sultry voice, and I had consented to have him manage my chaos for me. On the radio, I had heard him try and fail to produce that alchemy of order and stability out of unwieldy pain. I had to give him credit for trying.

This penchant for Christians to give advice on sexuality is as prevalent as the experience of wilderness itself. If you wander into any Christian bookstore or peruse Christian magazines, you'll find lots of such advice. Likewise, the Internet is full of "ministries" dedicated to the subject of sexuality, all intended as guides. On The Marriage Bed: Sex and Intimacy for Married Christians, an independent website that offers resources to married and engaged couples on the subject of sexuality, the authors try to answer that enduring question, "What is it right to do?" On a page called "Keeping Sexually Pure," a couple named "Tom and Catherine" give us a good overview of a commonly Christian way through the wilderness: make rules. Lots of rules. Keeping sexually pure means maintaining absolute control over one's desires. As an unmarried couple, Tom and Catherine advocate layers of rules. First, there are the "ground rules" that a couple must establish at the beginning of their relationship. Then there are the additional rules that become necessary as a couple grows in intimacy. Finally, Catherine confesses, as if she were a rule junkie with a stash, there are her own private rules that she adds "on top of the set we already have."

Tom and Catherine are like many Christians who imagine that Christian sex is not like secular sex, and that it is set apart by rules. Christian sex is safe and pure. Secular sex is dangerous and exploitative and leads on a path to destruction. One extreme example of this logic is found in an almost harrowing moment of Alexandra Pelosi's documentary *Friends of God*. Pelosi stands with the soon-to-be former pastor of New Life Church in Colorado Springs, Ted Haggard, just weeks before the scandal broke. They are poised at the entrance to the church when Haggard says with a wink, "You know, all the studies say that evangelicals have better sex than anyone else."

"Really?" Pelosi says from behind the camera.

Haggard gestures toward two young men from the church who are standing nearby. "How often do you have sex with your wives?" Haggard asks them.

"Every day," one of them jumps in, as if he knows the script. "Sometimes twice a day."

Haggard looks at the other man.

"Every day," he says nervously.

"And out of a hundred times that you have sex with your wife, how often does she climax?" Haggard asks.

"Every one," they say almost in unison. "Every one."

Haggard grins, wide and toothy. One of the young men feels obligated to explain this unlikely reality. "There's a natural order to things," he says. "The way God set it up is the best way to do things and that's the flat-out truth."

While Christian mythology teaches that Christian sex protects us from heartache and plants us squarely in God's order of things, the reality that most of us face is far different. Christianity does very little, if anything, to protect us from abuse, manipulation, objectification, and betrayal. Studies show that Christian teens engage in riskier sexual behavior than non-Christian teens. An abstinence pledge taken by a teenage girl delays a decision to have intercourse by six months. Pornography is used by more than half the men attending a Promise Keepers event. Christians divorce at a rate identical to or higher than the rest of the population. And so on.

This doesn't mean that "the rules" don't sometimes function properly and guide people onto solid ground. They certainly can. But they have become almost the only way that American Christians know how to talk about religion and sex, and these rules have left many people hungry to understand why they cannot place themselves on this map.

In part this is because Christian sex and secular sex, as they are imagined in popular culture, have far more in common than is generally recognized. Both the kind of sexuality found in media culture and the kind found in Christian culture function on a set of ideals to which their adherents can never live up. In media culture, these are generally standards of beauty. In Christian culture, they are standards of "purity" that involve excluding and denying sexual thoughts. Our anxiety about our inadequacy keeps us turning back for more—another product to help us feel more beautiful, a little closer to the standard, or another rule to edge ourselves toward God's ideal plan.

No one I interviewed for this book fit the ideal. All were broken, all had been hurt, all struggled to interpret their life experiences with very little help. Most wanted their names changed and details obscured because these stories were sensitive and contained secrets that the people around them didn't know—people they loved. All of these people were utterly ordinary; all of them spent time in the wilderness; some of them are still there. Sexuality and spirituality have yet to find an integrated form in their lives.

In the Christian tradition, the wilderness is an important place. While it is confusing, disorienting, and frightening, it is also a place where God can be met. In our wanderings, the tradition teaches us, God is present. Our experiences do not need to be read as a record of our failures to meet God's standards, but as a record of the ways that God has tried to reach us. In the Eastern Orthodox tradition of Christianity, worshippers hear the story of Saint Mary of Egypt, a fifth-century woman, every Lent. Saint Mary was a young girl who ran away from home at an early age and traveled to the city of Alexandria, where she survived by selling her body for sex, spinning flax, and begging. When she was twenty-nine, she decided to take a pilgrimage to Jerusalem, offering sexual favors to other pilgrims to pay her way. But in Jerusalem and later in Bethany, she had several experiences that began to change her. At a monastery on the banks of the Jordan, she heard a voice that said, "Cross over and you will find peace and rest." She took the voice literally, crossed the river into the wilderness on the other side, and lived there alone for many years.

One day, many years later, a monk was out praying in the desert when he saw what he thought was a ghost. He then realized that he was seeing a woman. Her skin was "scorched by the sun," and her hair was "sparse and woolly white." She ran away from him, but he pursued her.

"Are you a ghost?" he asked as he approached.

"No," she said. "I am altogether earth and ashes and flesh."

After he had given her his cloak, she told him her story and then asked him to bring her communion on the bank of the river on Holy Thursday. When he returned with a basket of figs and soaked lentils along with bread and wine, he saw her walking on the surface of the water toward him. She kissed him in greeting with "the kiss of love on his mouth." He fell to her feet and begged her to pray "for the Church, for the Empire, for him." Then he released her because he dared "not hold for long one who will not be held." When he returned again the next year with his basket, he found her lifeless body by the bank of the river, with a lion seated at her feet licking her soles.

When I first encountered this story of sexual and spiritual wilderness, I was riveted. I felt haunted by it. I was drawn to Mary's power and to her sorrow. Her sexuality seemed unreconciled and yet somehow still powerful and vivid. Her loneliness made me ache. I was struck by how her body was the source of her pain and less clearly, the source of her redemption. I was intrigued by her interaction with the monk and his passion for her.

But I still had no idea what to make of her story for contemporary people. A few years later, I was at a conference of writers and artists. It was a late summer evening, and people had gathered at picnic tables out on the deck. I overheard a woman farther down the table mention Saint Mary of Egypt. I moved so that I could be closer to her and listen in. This woman, a lesbian and an artist, had recently joined the Eastern Orthodox Church and had taken Saint Mary's name as her own spiritual name. When I asked her why, she said she saw in this story a picture of herself: a woman who had been scarred early by sexual abuse and who wandered restlessly seeking redemption and reconciliation.

So many of us have gone into exile in the wilderness, some by choice and some by force. For all the ways that we have cultivated our "spirituality," we have not found a way to meet our bodies as holy. Saint Mary of Egypt retains her power by her extreme aloneness. Yet the gestures she accepts—food, a kiss, the touching of her feet—hint that even she longs for embodied love. Her story is marked by ambivalence and unease. She has both transcendence and an unrelieved sadness. Part of me wants to join her in the wilderness. Part of me wants to wrap her in a blanket, end her exile, and bring her home.

Sarah

Sarah learned early how to be the kind of girl of whom her family could be proud. The oldest child in a family of Korean immigrants, she used her keen intelligence and her ear for language to translate for her mother. She was obedient and trustworthy and took care of her little brothers. Very quickly, she learned that one of the most important skills in her dual-culture, dual-language world was the ability to keep secrets.

Sarah's father was a Presbyterian minister who had been trained in Korea and had served a small church there when Sarah was a baby. When he was granted a scholarship to study theology at Princeton University in the United States, the family moved, and Sarah's earliest memories are of the dilapidated university housing and the narrow kitchen where her mother set out five-gallon buckets and spread newspaper on the floor to make kimchi.

From an early age, Sarah served as her mother's liaison. She knew everyone in the building: the law students, the seminarians, the quiet Chinese couple studying mathematics. She knew which apartments housed PhD students who came home late and slept in, appearing in the hallways on weekend mornings weary eyed and dazed.

Every word that Sarah spoke was a translation from one language to another. And she translated, not only with her mouth, but with her whole body. Every gesture was an attempt to bridge the divide between her traditional Korean home and the American world that surrounded it. Depending on the environment she entered and what was expected of her in it, she smiled differently, laughed differently, raised or lowered her voice, or used her hands for different kinds of gestures. Her ability to accommodate her new culture was so good that she could even adopt a slight New Jersey twang when she wanted one, but she felt like she was always trying to explain something to someone.

These constant translations became second nature to Sarah, but as the oldest daughter, she was acutely aware of her mother's struggles. Both the English language and American culture were difficult for her mother to grasp. Sarah's mother expressed admiration for Americans. She saw them as a strong, willful, even stubborn people, who made their lives what they wanted them to be, in contrast with Koreans who often believed that fate had predetermined their course. She was grateful for the opportunities that her adopted country gave her husband and children. At the same time, she found American culture baffling and frightening. People were aggressive and intense. All the television and newspapers and magazines advertised sex day and night, and she worried about the effect that would have on her children. She ached for Korea, where her mother and her sisters lived, where the seafood was fresher and the peppers hotter. To come to America, she had given up her role as her mother's dutiful daughter and closest ally. That caused her pain every day.

Sarah's mother carried a strong sense of *han*—a Korean word that means duty, suffering, and sacrifice. It was a sense that she had inherited from her own mother who had in turn inherited it from hers. She intended to convey it Sarah, her only daughter, because it was the essence of

Korean womanhood. Your life is not your own to do with what you want. It belongs to others—to family, to those who have gone before you, to your community, to God.

In Korean culture, people have a place, and Sarah's responsibility was to take her place, and like her mother, sacrifice, even suffer, to fulfill her duty. In Sarah's mother's case, this sacrifice took the form of longing for her homeland. She expressed both her responsibility and her yearning in the simplest ways—quiet sighs that spoke volumes or grimly set expressions, as well as lectures on proper behavior and sharp comments about Sarah's misdeeds.

Sarah's mother tried to make their home into a small oasis of Korean culture. All the food she cooked and served was traditional. Celebrations were conducted by formal customs that she remembered from her childhood. On Saturdays, she conscripted Sarah into hours of service making sweet potato noodles. Summer afternoons were often spent at the park where the Korean Christian community gathered for barbecues, and Sarah watched her mother relax in the familiarity of culture and language. To friends, neighbors, distant relatives, people from the university, graduate students from across the hall, and people in the church, Sarah's mother provided almost constant hospitality. For every guest, the house was cleaned, the carpets steamed, the couch vacuumed. Even when no one was coming for supper, Sarah's mother prepared platters of *guksu* and steamed buns for Sarah to deliver spontaneously to neighbors. In this way, her mother stayed quietly, even mutely, connected to the world around her, nourishing it in the best way she knew how.

The family valued two things, perhaps above all else: connections to others and appearances. The family name was paramount, and everyone needed to work to keep it up.

Sarah often blushed to hear her parents brag of her accomplishments to relations in Korea, even exaggerate them, and their pride in her had the odd effect of making her feel ashamed. At the same time, she found herself telling them things that she knew would please them while concealing her failures to avoid their disapproval. The family currency was honor—the goal to accumulate it, sometimes at the cost of truth. Even though Sarah did excel and did bring honor to the family, she often felt it wasn't enough. She sensed in her mother a trenchant sadness. That sadness was her sacrifice. For her husband and children, she had given up Korea, her home, her family. Sometimes Sarah felt resentful that she couldn't take that sadness away. She felt angry that her mother didn't work harder to learn English and integrate into American society. And yet, wordlessly, she accepted her mother's ancient burden, the one passed down from one generation to the next—the one that would be hers.

Sarah's father, on the other hand, had a flamboyant, jovial personality. At the university, he had friends of every race, color, religion, and background. His English, while imperfect, was in constant use for making jokes and giving unsolicited advice, especially on the subject of religion and morality. While his secular neighbors may not have appreciated his spontaneous lectures, everyone genuinely seemed to like him. He held his Korean identity lightly and his Christianity passionately. He believed that the whole world needed the saving light of Jesus Christ, and his sermons invariably played on this theme.

But her father also had his shadow side, his own secrets. The responsibility to be successful, to build an American life for his family, to show off for his colleagues or report his successes back home could weigh heavily. Sometimes, he returned to the apartment long after bedtime, and Sarah could hear the muffled sounds of her parents arguing.

After he finished his doctorate of ministry degree, the family moved four times to three states while her father served churches of various sizes, ethnic makeups, and needs. He settled, when Sarah was ten, at a large church in a suburb where there were few Koreans. The constant moving meant that Sarah entered new schools almost every year. She was an excellent adapter, but she was also often lonely.

As an adolescent, Sarah felt the distance between Korean culture and American culture acutely. On the one hand, she could freely partake of American culture whenever she was outside her home, without her parents ever knowing. She could watch movies at a friend's house that her parents would never let her see. She could learn all the words to songs she knew her parents would hate. On the other hand, family love and duty and the potential for betrayal and disappointment loomed large. Sarah was good at being who her parents needed her to be. She was good at performing at church, at home, and in school.

Of all her mother's fear and warnings about the permissiveness of American culture, dating was number one. In her mother's version of Korean culture, no dating was allowed in high school (or even in college, but that was a problem for a later time). Who touched whom and when, what happened in public, how girls dressed—these were guided by strict rules, codes governed by propriety and modesty, a sense of honor, piety, and righteousness that were irrefutable. It wasn't merely a case of cultures clashing or of Sarah finding her way between them. In this case, Korean culture clearly trumped American culture. Sarah would be kept safe. She would not date, nor be allowed to spend time in contexts and with people who threatened this code. (Years later, Sarah traveled to Korea and laughed at how old-fashioned her parents' version of the immutable rules of Korean culture were. She saw young women dressed in the tiniest halter tops and young couples making out on the benches. The youth culture she saw bore little resemblance to the one that her parents had so firmly espoused.)

Sarah observed closely the contrast with American culture. Her friends' relationships with their parents seemed considerably looser and freer. When her friends talked about being "close" with their parents, they meant that they could talk with their parents about anything, or so they claimed. Sarah thought about the innumerable things that she could and would not talk with her mother about and wondered, "Are we close?" And yet she felt connected to her mother and to her family by bonds that far exceeded words, by a loyalty that could not be spoken. She did not perceive this fundamental loyalty to family among her American friends. Her friends were freer to disobey, freer to make their own choices or to challenge the rules, and yet that freedom came at a cost.

Adolescence also brought a dark time to Sarah's home. Her parents argued frequently, even when they put on happy faces to go to church. They each seemed to be building and keeping grudges against each other, creating blame for circumstances neither of them could control. Sarah reflected later that if it had not been for "family honor" and for the very public position of her father as a pastor, her family might have blown apart under the pressure. Sometimes, Sarah wonders if that would have been a good thing. As it was, her parents often seemed to clench their teeth in order to walk into church smiling.

In perhaps the worst incident, Sarah's father's elderly mother came for a long anticipated visit from Korea. Before she came, their split-level suburban home was scrubbed from top to bottom, but Sarah's father was still critical of throw pillows that had frayed edges or a swipe of dust under a lamp. Sarah's grandmother stayed for several months, and with each passing day the tension between her mother and father seemed to rise. One day, Sarah's mother was helping her mother-in-law to the car for a grocery shopping errand when her grandmother slipped and broke her ankle. Her father blamed her mother for carelessness and thought-lessness, even hinting that she had deliberately provoked the incident. Another time, an uncle mysteriously and suddenly died, and there was a hush around his death that was full of something ominous. Years later, Sarah finally heard the word *suicide* in relation to his death. Her family seemed to hold secrets within secrets within secrets, a labyrinth of things not said.

In junior high, Sarah and her friends went crazy over certain boy bands and collected posters of Britney Spears and other pop music icons. Sarah joined in the various crazes as enthusiastically as she knew how, but all of them seemed to underline the same point: Sarah was different. Their idols were all blond and buxom. Everywhere she went, Sarah was one of only a handful of Asians. She felt constantly that she was not and would never be desirable or beautiful.

At the same time, it was perfectly clear that to be desirable, to be one of the girls that boys wrote notes about or gave presents to, would be frowned upon at home. By being invisible at school, Sarah could save herself a lot of trouble.

Once in the seventh grade, a friend of Sarah's wore a halter top and short shorts to a school picnic. Sarah's mother never let the subject drop: if her daughter went out in public dressed like that, the shame on the entire family would be unimaginable. The message from her family was, "Don't screw this up. A lot of people have sacrificed a lot to give you the opportunities they never had."

Sarah sensed that she was lagging behind everyone else, as if the strict Christian community with its rules and piety and her Korean family with its sense of shame and propriety were a set of heavy weights around her ankles. Her parents' rules for high school were firm: no dating, an early curfew, observation of her every move. Everyone else, so it seemed to Sarah, was gallivanting toward adulthood—dating, gossiping, kissing—while she slogged along with protections that seemed increasingly painful and useless. As far as she could tell, her parents' plan was to keep her locked up until she was a piece of rotting fruit and then would take her around to find a husband for her. The thought was abhorrent to her, but she also felt trapped. "I thought my parents were so off," Sarah said. "I thought they just didn't know anything about American culture."

Like many children of immigrants, identity was a major source of conflict for Sarah. "Am I American?" Sarah asked herself constantly. "Or am I Korean? Will I ever belong anywhere?" She felt the constant tug of war, and for a long time neither side seemed to be winning.

In the summer before Sarah's senior year of high school, her mother's mother came for her first visit from Korea. Sarah had long heard stories about her grandmother, stories of both admiration and caution, stories that seemed to have been offered as an explanation for the reality that Sarah found herself in. Her grandmother was a person that her mother revered. She had lived through three wars. Her father and brother had been killed by the Japanese. The family had known extreme poverty and had been close to starvation. Through it all, her grandmother had lived a devout life, had raised four children, and had sacrificed herself for others. That sense of *han* was embodied in the bent, beautiful, frail flesh of her grandmother. At the same time, in part because of how hard her grandmother's life had been, Sarah's own mother had chosen to raise her children in the United States, where they might have ease, more opportunities, where the burden of history might not be so heavy. Sarah was glad that her grandmother was coming; she hoped unconsciously, that if she saw her and got to know her, she might know which part of her was truly Korean.

But it wasn't, of course, that simple. Sarah loved her grandmother and could see her strength, her gentleness, and her gracious hospitality. At the same time, there were a lot of things she did that Sarah found just plain irritating. Her presence stirred up for Sarah's mother all kinds of guilt and regret. She was sorry that her mother was living alone in Korea without her oldest daughter's help. She lived in fear that if her mother got sick, she would not be there. That fear took the form of excessive care, brooding, hovering over Sarah's grandmother. Sarah's mother was anxious about showing her mother every aspect of their life. She worried that the house was too nice; it would shame her mother. Or maybe it wasn't nice enough—it would make their bragging seem small. The layers of her mother's fear and anxieties weighed heavily on Sarah, as they always had. Although she and her mother now fought constantly, it still felt like her mother's feelings had a direct line into Sarah's veins. The presence of Sarah's grandmother increased tension between Sarah's parents and made the entire family dynamic play at a higher pitch.

As fighting with her mother intensified, Sarah felt her longing for freedom more acutely, along with terror at what freedom would cost. She and her mother fought about what her grandmother thought or didn't think, about Sarah's clothing or nonexistent attention from boys, friends, church, school, the flute—anything and everything was an opportunity to vent their frustrations on each other. Sarah frequently stormed out of the house to sit on her little brother's swing set and cry.

One of the things that Sarah and her mother argued about was whether Sarah should take a job at the local mall. Without her parents' consent, she went to the Cinnabon counter and applied. She got the job and, eventually, won the right to take it. In painstaking negotiations with her parents, Sarah agreed to work the morning shift so that she would not be driving home from the mall in the dark. She would still make state orchestra rehearsals, and she would never put in more than fifteen hours a week.

It was a hard won freedom, and Sarah relished it. Every morning she arrived early and entered the mall through a side door where the employees' locker and break room was. She walked through the smoky lounge to put on her apron. Then she walked the still quiet halls of the mall to the food court where she entered through an inner door and finally to the Cinnabon counter.

When she had been in junior high, the mall had been a place of refuge and her first place of freedom. She'd gone there with her friends on Saturday afternoons. They bought earrings and ice cream and occupied a table at the food court where they could talk about everyone who walked by. The smell of the mall—sweet, sticky, new, plasticky—suggested that a person could be anything she wanted to be, that the possibilities were endless, that desires could be answered, that identities could be fluidly connected. Sarah felt, wordlessly, that the mall was the place where the longings in her could be reconciled if she just bought the right things.

Now opening the Cinnabon by herself also suggested a delicious freedom. She felt responsible and mature. She knew her boss liked and trusted her, that she was thrilled to have her working the morning shift every day of the summer. She didn't know any of the other employees at the mall, and she was shy. She kept to herself and passed through the employees' lounge without talking to anyone. She didn't have any stories of recent hangovers; she didn't drink the burned coffee in the lounge or smoke cigarettes.

But nearly every day, when she went to her locker, there was a boy sitting on the couch watching her. He would give her a quick, shy smile. "He has nice teeth," she thought. Definitely his best feature. Otherwise, he was skinny with long bangs that hung over his eyes and a pocked complexion. At first, she did not smile back, not even sure the smile was intended for her, but eventually she did.

His name was Jacob, and he worked in mall maintenance. He made a point of coming by her counter in the morning to empty the trash near her booth, just to say hello, even when the trash can wasn't full. Eventually, Jacob asked her out. She said no. But all day after she said no, her heart pounded, and she chastised herself. Was she a snob? Jacob was the first boy who had ever paid attention to her, and she treated him like dirt. He liked her. That was exciting in itself and seemed to merit a response. What was wrong with going on a date with someone? Did it matter that they were so different?

What happened next was not logical or predictable, but when Sarah looked back on it, she wondered if it might not have been inevitable. She was in a state of pure rebellion against her parents, their culture, and their religion. Jacob was the perfect vehicle for that rebellion. When Jacob asked her out again, she said, "Sure." But she didn't tell him where she lived. She made arrangements to meet him near the mall and lied to her parents about where she was going. They went to a movie and afterward got a Coke at McDonald's. Another time, they went to a diner and sat in the vinyl booth without talking. She always felt like they were playacting, imagining what other people did or said on dates and awkwardly trying to do the same. A couple of times, Jacob took her to his house where he lived with his mother. It was a sad-looking place, a narrow, brick, row house with a weedy, neglected yard. As far as Sarah could tell, Jacob's mother never left the house. She didn't work and was always dressed in a faded housecoat and slippers. The house had a moldy, neglected smell. The few times that Sarah went there, she stood in the kitchen shifting from foot to foot, wanting desperately to leave.

After lying to her parents about where she was, Sarah would spend the entire evening worrying that they would try to track her down. She was careful never to mention Jacob's name to anyone else she knew. Oddly she was not interested in romance, and she wasn't even sure she liked Jacob. She appreciated the fact that he seemed to like her, and it was exciting to do something so far outside her parents' approval. But romance was not the path to freedom that she sought, and she saw little in Jacob to be romantic about.

One weekend, Sarah's parents took her brothers and grandmother to a family church retreat on the Jersey shore. Her mother stocked the refrigerator with food for Sarah to heat up after work and told Sarah she would call every night to check in. As soon as they were gone, Sarah invited Jacob to come over. He came, almost dutifully. She showed him around her house, and then she took him upstairs to her bedroom. He sat on the edge of her bed, looked at her posters, her photos, her desk, her stuffed animals. She pushed aside the thought that came into her mind—that Jacob looked wrong sitting on her bed. She chastised herself again, as she had many times in the few weeks that she had been spending time with Jacob, for being elitist, for judging him.

But then he patted the place on the bed next to him. She could feel her insides turn to water. Panic rose. How had she gotten here, she wondered, although the answer seemed pitifully clear: she had come here entirely by her own will and of her own choice. She swallowed hard. She didn't want Jacob to think that she was a scared little girl. She didn't want her fear to show. She didn't want him to know that now having him sit on her bed made her feel sick. She sat down next to him.

He kissed her. He seemed to know exactly what he was doing, as if had done this many times before. "I should just go along with this," she thought. "This is totally normal. It's no big deal. It's what everyone does." When he pushed her back on the bed, her mind went blank, and she thought of nothing more until "it" was over. She had sex with Jacob on her bed in her little bedroom of her parents' house. Or, as she later put it to herself, "He had sex with me, and I let him."

But as soon as it was over, a wave of powerful self-disgust overtook her. "I want you to leave," she said. "Now."

She was home alone for the next two days. She called in sick to work. She took four or five showers. She washed the sheets and the comforter from her bed. She felt that she had dirtied her parents' home, dirtied herself, and there was no way to get clean. When her parents came home, she was quiet. Her mother opened the refrigerator and said, "You didn't eat *anything*," in a scolding tone. "I wasn't that hungry," she said.

For a week afterward, Sarah told no one, harboring the story like a secret that she only half believed herself. She avoided everything about Jacob at the mall. She took a different route into work, and when she caught sight of him out of the corner of her eye, she felt nauseous. Finally, she told her best friend, a girl to whom she had never spoken a word about Jacob. She told her the whole ugly story and waited for Meredith to look at her like she was an alien. She felt like she was handing Meredith a sack of stinking garbage and asking her to hold it. But Meredith held the story gently. She listened and tried to help Sarah make sense of it. After that, Sarah felt a little lighter.

For Sarah's entire life, her parents had taught her—and not only taught her, but demonstrated in every gesture—that sex was sacred. When two people had sex, they weren't just two bodies touching; they were truly connected spiritually, emotionally, and physically. Sarah felt she had traded in—she didn't know how to put it to herself—her sacred purity, her self, or some very precious part of herself. What had she gotten in return? Anyone who truly cared about Sarah would be horrified by what she had done. She could hardly look at herself in the mirror. That person seemed like a stranger.

At the same time, other realizations were creeping in, as if having sex with Jacob had awakened her from a long dream. For one thing, having sex with Jacob had accomplished a goal she didn't know she'd made: it had created a breach with her parents. Now the course of her life and the course of theirs were very different. Sarah was not the same obedient girl she had always been. If, at the beginning of the summer, her rebellion had been in words, it was now decidedly in deeds.

Because the breach had now been created, Sarah went back to her old submissive ways. There was no longer any reason to argue. She started school, put in an application for a job at a clothing store at the mall, and made plans for college. She made all state orchestra, second chair. She submitted applications and scholarship forms as if filling out paperwork for a person she no longer was. She went to church as always, though it had become something very distant from her. She took steps to avoid conflict with her mother, afraid of what would come out of her mouth if she opened it in anger. She felt she needed time to understand what this breach meant, and she needed quiet to do that. Her mother, with relief, took the change as a sign of Sarah's growing maturity.

After long reflection, another realization came: as much as having sex with Jacob had been a terrible mistake, and as much as she regretted it, it had ended something in Sarah that needed ending. As soon as it was over, she had awakened to a truer self than the one who had gone out with Jacob in the first place. She had been heading, all but deliberately, down that path, believing that she had to have sex with someone, really anyone, to become a part of

American culture. No one and nothing had contradicted that understanding, and she had imagined it to be crucial. Now she knew that wasn't true. Why she always had to do the wrong thing first in order to learn it was wrong, she didn't know. But that was a fact. It was a gruesome fact. It was a lesson that had to be lived, however unpleasant.

The question of who to be now took on greater urgency, as two versions of Sarah now lay behind her. For example, what should she make of her parents' faith? During her crisis, church had been of no help to her. It had been one more place to perform an old Sarah. Church was a place where her father shone, and the whole family was fully invested in helping him shine. Truly, she wanted that for him. The importance of it was something she had felt her whole life; it lived in her bones. All her family life hinged on that, and she hated to think what their family would be like without his success. But in her own mind and heart, she could feel a growing coldness toward Christianity. None of it meant much to her personally. She supposed that she believed in God, but it was hard to see what difference that made.

In college, away from her parents' daily observation, Sarah created two separate identities. In one, she was free to act like everyone else, to try on ways of being in the world that was not her parents'. She was not Korean. She was just Sarah. She went to parties, developed friendships, studied—and while she wanted to bring honor to her family with good grades, she didn't have to work so hard to keep up her image.

On the other hand, Sarah did not want to create any more anxiety for her parents than she already had. She not only brought home good grades, she created an identity that she could bring home as well. When she arrived at college, she quickly scanned the available churches, picked one, and attended once, just to learn the pastor's name and what kinds of groups they had for young people. That way, when her parents called, she could tell them where she had decided to go to church. But she knew that she wouldn't go, or if she did, it would be rarely. She felt guilty about lying to her parents about something they held so sacred, especially as it became obvious to her that she really had no intention of going to church. But the price of the truth was too high.

Her distance from Christianity grew. She did not describe herself as a Christian, and she rarely thought about religion and religious beliefs. But she could see the impact of her upbringing on her choices. She felt compelled to find meaningful work and began taking environmental science classes with a passion. She realized that her struggle over her identity gave her an innate felicity with other cultures; she connected easily with people from all over the world and had friends from many countries.

College held a number of surprises. Among them was the final death of the idea that she had lagged far behind everyone else in coming to grips with her identity and sexuality. One afternoon, sitting around with some girls from her high school who were at the same university, she learned that none of them had had sex in high school. Not one. Her own "sexual experience" with Jacob, that one nightmarish afternoon, gave her more experience than any of them. That fact seemed ironic and strange. Her perception of American culture had been wrong.

Still, she thought, if it hadn't been Jacob, it would have been someone else. That afternoon had taught her not how to be more like her peers, but how to be more like herself. The questions raised by that encounter were still burning, and answers continued to elude her. What of Koreanness would she carry forward? Would some meaningful sense of Christianity return to her or would she just go through the motions to please her parents? What does being American mean? And in the midst of all of this, what is sex? "I still don't know where to put sex in my categorization of things," Sarah admits, years after the incident with Jacob and after other boyfriends and sexual experiences. Sex, while relentlessly defined by both culture and religion, still somehow escapes them.

In college she "hooked up" a few times at parties, an experience that was too frighteningly similar to what had happened with Jacob. She started dating someone seriously, keeping his existence a secret from her parents for a long time, and tried to imagine what it would be like to marry him. Then she broke up with him and fled on a semester trip abroad working on water quality issues in Bolivia. During those months, the hallway of the youth hostel was traffic for everyone sharing everyone else's beds. The boundaries between right and wrong, good and bad, seemed to dissolve completely, and Sarah remembers it with a kind of swimming unreality.

Every step along the way deepened the paradox of Sarah's situation. Each step took her farther from her parents' world, deeper into a no-man's-land that had dimensions she could not fathom. And yet, each step has also underlined her core commitments to her family, the inescapability of *han*, the true ties of love for her parents.

One seed of an answer to Sarah's questions about her identity may lie in her mother's hospitality. That core goodness, that endless giving, seems to soften all the hard edges and temper the demons of culture and religion. Her mother gave freely without concern for where those who received came from. Hospitality—if one could offer it to oneself and to others—might be a way of moving forward even when other pictures weren't clear.

While Sarah is not ready to say that sex is sacred, she does think of it as special, something that should be reserved and considered carefully. She would love to go back and tell her younger self, "Don't do it with a douche bag." The American culture that Sarah had once longed to be a part of seemed to teach that sex was a necessary part of self-expression. But Sarah now questions that proposition, as she questions much of what she received as "American." Sarah wasn't exactly expressing herself when she had sex with Jacob. There was very little of herself in that act. She never asked herself any questions about pleasure or desire. She never asked what she wanted from the relationship or why. She just acted out a very poorly written script, a bad movie. The thought that she used Jacob and was used in return still sometimes hurts.

In her haste to detach sex and herself from its oppressive cultural, religious, and familial meanings, she plunged herself deep into the wilderness, a place in which her life experience has only grown richer, more complex, where her questions daily grow less easy to answer.

Mark

To the dinner table most nights, Mark's father, a Methodist minister, brought theology. Sometimes it was subtle, sometimes explicit. In the most ordinary experiences of life, Mark's father saw an opportunity to reflect on deeper meanings and deeper purposes, on how to guide one's life onto the right path and into a deeper relationship with God. He didn't always bring questions or even answers; it was more of an orientation, a way of seeing the world that Mark breathed in. It took up residence in his cells. Life, his father's bearing said, has meaning. That meaning is to live every moment overseen by and in relation to a loving but stern and deeply involved God, who wants to see us ordered according to his plan and living out our best possible lives.

The books on his father's shelves likewise suggested that the moral and religious life was the product of hard work, discipline, and study, just as deeply intellectual as it was relational. In their wealthy suburb of Cincinnati, Mark's family was by no means rich. They lived modestly, strove to do good in their community, and strove to offer their children a strong, Christian environment. Mark's father had come from a more conservative tradition than the one he practiced now. He founded the church that he served and attempted to meld together traditional theology and vibrant faith. He was able to convey his learning to the people of his church with passion and grace. The people of the church in return loved him and loved his family.

For Mark and his siblings, the church was a second home. They played hide-and-seek in the pews and knew where every door led and the contents of every storage closet. They ate leftover communion bread and drank the juice.

By the time Mark was in junior high, two of his older siblings had already passed through the Young Life group that his parents supported. They were moving on to Christian colleges. Young Life was a national organization almost fifty years old by the time Mark participated. It had thousands of chapters in the United States, several summer camps in every region of the country, and a strong national leadership. Mark's parents had incorporated Young Life into the ministry of the church and made it central to youth.

Every Young Life meeting started with mixers—skits, games, icebreakers. Then the leaders would begin to play music, indicating a transition to a more serious time of reflection. Usually, the guitar music would start loud and dynamic to match the mood of the games and then gradually shift into softer and more meditative tones. One of the leaders would have prepared a talk, drawn from his or her own experience, that almost always focused in one way or another on the reality of sin and the need for redemption.

Mark attended so many of these sessions that they became axiomatic for him. Their rhythm was no longer the rhythm of an organization skilled at working with young people; it was the very rhythm of righteousness, a way of following an inner light toward the right way of living. It brought the inner and the outer life together. It helped shape life according to God's plan. And "God's plan for your life" was a constant theme. God intended for young people to "live lives worthy of him"—lives of purity with training in character. Eventually, according to God's plan, they would form Christian marriages, find meaningful work, and raise children trained in the same way. All of this felt right to Mark, perfectly right.

Mark was in early adolescence when the talk at Young Life first turned to sexuality. The most important point conveyed by the youth leaders was that waiting to have sex until you were married was paramount, an important component in God's plan, an essential ingredient to a holy life. In early high school, the leaders would split boys and girls into separate groups to discuss these things. The conversations were meant to serve as guideposts and warnings on the precious road of life. Sexual behavior was presented— or at least Mark perceived it—as a continuum of actions. It began with physical attraction and harmless activities like holding hands. But then the continuum became an increasingly slippery slope with kissing poised at the precipice and "everything else" leading directly to intercourse. Intercourse was the ultimate sin with terrible consequences for the unmarried. Intercourse outside of marriage was a clear violation of God's plan. All of the other activities— kissing, fondling, touching, murky areas that Mark knew little about—were dangerous primarily because they could lead to intercourse and because they were giving in to the lower desires of the body instead of the higher desires for God. Beyond that, they were taught that sexuality was a "great gift" that could easily be used wrongly.

When Mark was in early adolescence and first heard this view of sexuality, it seemed to be God's purpose to keep people safe from their own sinful natures. The thought of doing anything with a girl beyond kissing was terrifying anyway. Holding hands, or perhaps kissing, sounded, in theory, like enough. Growing up in the 1990s, Mark had plenty of opportunity to observe examples of famous people who chose to live outside of God's plan. He was still in junior high when Monica Lewinsky and Bill Clinton had "sex" in the Oval Office. The disgust of Mark's parents was vivid to him. Mark clearly remembers Clinton's denial: "I did not have sex with that woman," and the revelation that the kind of sex he had was oral. His parents were derisive. Oral sex is sex. Betrayal is betrayal. Adultery is adultery. Mark remembers the moment in part because it helped him put oral sex more explicitly on his moral continuum. He placed it at the bottom of the steep slope, just before intercourse under an imaginary headline labeled "sex." Knowing that sex outside of marriage is wrong, he knew that oral sex is also fornication, and thus displeasing to God.

One of the television shows that Mark watched growing up was *Dawson's Creek*, a show about four teenagers living in a fictitious seaside town in Massachusetts. The teens were all white, beautiful, and obsessed with the question of sex. One central theme of the show was coming of age through sexuality, a necessary part of growing up. It was something that people did to express themselves, to manipulate others, to wound, or to connect. Sex—whether characters were having sex or not having sex—was a significant undercurrent of the show.

While this couldn't have been more different from Mark's own experience or from what he had been taught, he recognized the way that image played a key role. This was equally true in Mark's church. Being beautiful and successful mattered a great deal. Mark was beginning to play the guitar for Young Life events, so he was gradually singled out to perform the role of ideal Christian young man for others. It was different than *Dawson's Creek*, to be sure, but performance of a particular image became central to his experience in the church.

Mark grew up with loving parents in a dynamic church with a Christian worldview imparted with both playfulness and reverence. It was insular enough that Mark felt these boundaries clearly, and not so much that it was suffocating, at least not for a long time. It provided him a solid place to stand. In many ways, Mark's upbringing was ideally Christian, in some of the best ways our culture can imagine.

Because living out an ideal Christian life hinged on marriage, sexual formation was a critical part of religious formation, even if it was rarely talked about. It was as if the "right path" was illuminated by floodlights. All a person had to do was follow that path toward righteousness, salvation, intimacy, and bliss.

From the time he was small, Mark had an inclination to please people. He wanted to do what other people thought was right—his parents, church people, teachers, his peers. Because God's guidance did not come literally, he looked to others for signs for how well he was doing. He cared that people said, "Mark is a great guy. What a fine young man." He formed himself accordingly. He had the right answers. He took the stage at church. He was handsome, athletic, and musically talented. He did well in school. Youth group girls fell in love with him; youth group boys looked up to him. He wasn't just Mark, one of the guys. He set the standard higher and pointed the way.

Embedded in the Young Life ritual is an intimate quality intended to arouse young people's emotions. After a time of laughter and play, the music intentionally transforms the mood of the group. "Praise singing" begins to lead a participant toward reflection that can be emotionally vulnerable and is intended to be. The person leading the singing, usually a man with a guitar, begins to turn inward as if beginning a private, interior conversation that other people are allowed to watch. He models the inward turn that everyone is supposed to take, but at the same time, he offers a visual example of what a relationship with God looks like.

Done well, an erotic element enters into this worshipful time that goes unrecognized, but allows people to feel powerfully connected to something larger than themselves. They begin to yearn for God, for each other, for a connection they can't quite name. The flirtatious relationships and physical play have prepared them to enter this place of greater intimacy. No one, of course, calls this activity erotic, and if they did, almost everyone would flee. But by erotic, I mean a powerful attractive force is put into play, one that stands apart from sexual touch, but that is still rooted in physical and emotional longing. This longing can have multiple objects: the longing to belong, to be a part of something beautiful, to connect one's whole self to something spiritual, but the most direct object for this desire is the person holding the guitar, an embodied example of the connection sought. American Christianity has rooted itself deeply in this power of attraction with all of its dangers and promises.

This is not an easy dynamic to do well, but Mark's youth group did. It functioned on the principle that Christian young people should be just as successful and attractive as anyone in the "world," but in addition they should also be strong in faith and righteousness. *Dawson's Creek* without the sex. The purpose of the Christian life was, in part, to equip people with the proper gear to judge themselves and others according to a very high set of standards.

For an adolescent, the dynamic that flowed from judgment easily followed: pity and rejection for those who failed to meet the standard (including oneself), admiration and even jealousy for those who appeared to attain a higher standard effortlessly. Mark habitually judged himself and others, and feared not meeting various standards of "cool."

When Mark was in high school, he finally had the opportunity to put his sexual mores into direct practice, and that was when the system started, ever so slightly, to crack. Mark dated a girl in the youth group, who was everything he thought she should be: pretty, smart, athletic, and committed to her faith. Mark was prepared to practice "kissing, hugging, holding hands," as the right way to handle a new romance. But there were times when he and Brenda were alone that the standards so clearly articulated seemed to fan out into a broad gray expanse. Black and white disappeared. Brenda did not seem to have internalized the standards as Mark had. She appeared, although they were too shy to talk about it, to be open to other things, and Mark could feel himself on the steep, slippery slope of the continuum, poised for a descent.

In response, he hardened himself. He and Brenda developed a dynamic. They would go a little "too far," touching in a way that went beyond the prescribed formula. Or was it too far? The line around kissing blurred, in ways that were both frightening and invigorating. He tried to fight back toward clarity, to scramble back up the slope. So he put distance between himself and Brenda, withdrawing to protect himself and Brenda from these powerful feelings, while he tried to straighten out his head. Brenda felt rejected and withdrew as well. Mark felt sorry for hurting her, and he continued to desire her, so he reached out for her again.

When withdrawing into himself didn't seem to work, Mark tried breaking the rules into smaller and smaller pieces in order to define exactly what could and couldn't be done. Maybe touching with clothes on is OK, but being naked is not. Maybe touching above the waist is OK, touching below is not. The more he negotiated the rules, the more the next step on the continuum presented itself as justifiable. What was "pure enough"? Yet he hated himself for justifying anything. The rules were not available for negotiation. Or were they?

The words used in church for sex—fornication and adultery—were so charged it was hard to hear them without feeling overwhelmed with shame. Whatever they meant, to whatever specific acts they referred, it could only be bad. The crude language Mark heard at school added to Mark's sense that his parents were right—the world didn't know how to treat sex as sacred. The logic he perceived, though it was a long time before he had language for it, went something like this: in the locker room world, girls were objects to be collected or exploited. A girl was not a person so much as she was an object that, if conquered or convinced, could be used to gratify you physically.

While it seemed obvious to Mark that the locker room logic was much more dehumanizing to girls than the church world, both taught him to see sexuality as disconnected from relationships. In both cases, girls were objects whose primary purpose was to provide physical gratification. In one case, that was allowed; in the other, it was forbidden. The two frameworks he had both seemed ill-fitting: sex as victory, sex as failure. That left the realm of touch that he shared with Brenda languageless. It was a shadowy, more dreamlike world, the secret realm of sensation and touch. It was the world of the body—what the body wanted, perceived, felt. Mark was supposed to, he knew, subdue and tame it with his will, but the process was subject to such repeated failure that the question of who was manipulating whom was a legitimate one. Mark had to demand ever more control over his animalistic, hedonistic self and keep his will functioning at a high level. Yet the secret world of touch was deep, warm, and compelling.

Mark remembers, in particular, an evening in the basement of his friend Tim's house when their Young Life leader, Aaron, led the boys in a discussion about sex. His goal was to help the boys affirm the standards. Mark looked around at the boys in the group, and he knew that many of them were doing things with their girlfriends that they were not going to say. Instead they all agreed: it is right, good, and holy to uphold a high standard, not to set oneself on a dangerous path. In the intimacy of the Young Life circle, it didn't feel like hypocrisy to say one thing while doing another. Instead, it felt like trying to get footing. The conversation was never presented as an open question anyway. The standards weren't available for discussion. The only question was whether a person was going to conform or not, and if not, what would be the consequences? Guilt? Shame? Setting a poor example to others? All of these were the source of worry. Sometimes during these conversations, Mark felt repentant: from this point forward, he and Brenda would only kiss. They would only go on public dates; they wouldn't linger in the car when Mark dropped her off. Other times, he argued with Aaron in his mind and felt rebellious. Sometimes he just felt confused.

Mark was a talented runner, and he received a running scholarship to a large state university. He could feel his parents' hesitancy even as he contemplated that option. His older siblings had already gone ahead of him to a Christian college with a good academic reputation. One of them was just about to graduate, was engaged to be married, and appeared to be successfully entering Christian adult life. He felt that was his parents' ideal for him as well, even if it went unstated. His mother tried not to say much about it, but Mark knew that she was terrified by stories she had heard about the state university—about the culture of binge drinking and hookups. Even if Mark successfully navigated that, why would he choose that poverty of experience, the loneliness and isolation, over a Christian college where he would find people who shared his values? She never said, "Don't go to the state university." That wasn't like her. But her delicacy around the issue and her desire to make sure he made his own decision, but made the right one, led Mark to the Christian college. He valued, more than anything, his parents' opinion of him, and he felt they had wisdom to offer.

The summer after his senior year, Mark, Brenda, and others from the youth group traveled to the Young Life camp in upstate New York. Around a campfire one night, with the sound of the Saranac River rushing past, Aaron, the Young Life leader that Mark had known for years and with whom he had been closest, confessed to the group that he had had sex with a girlfriend in college. This spring, he had gotten engaged to a different woman. He deeply regretted that he could not give himself for the first time to his wife. He urged the young people around the campfire not to make the same mistake. It was one of his biggest regrets. Even though Aaron knew that God had forgiven him, he could not forgive himself.

Everyone felt chastened after the emotional campfire and Aaron's tears. It was rare to hear a story told so vulnerably by someone they had so long known and admired. They felt tender toward Aaron. They wanted to extend to him the forgiveness that he could not give himself. But they also knew the take-home message. The point was that now they were warned: this regret could be theirs. Avoiding it was paramount to purity. Mark could not meet Brenda's eyes. He stayed in his own private thoughts.

Looking back on that campfire and his upbringing, Mark wonders about the inability to talk openly about sex. He felt a profound disconnect between his experience and the ideal that was set before him. Sex could be joked about or it could be talked about the way Aaron had: as an object of regret, successfully interpreted and put away. "We could talk about sex or girls relatively easily, but when it came to imagining what those relationships might look like morally, that was less easy. We could use humor; we could recite codes; but we had a hard time seeing morality as a creative task." Mark found that he could conform to the ideal, basically, especially if his girlfriend agreed it was necessary. "But the girl became an objective, a way to prove myself, instead of a person."

At college, Mark observed couples who were having sex and not talking about it. He saw couples who had decided not even to kiss until the altar, in pursuit of the ideal, but also, in some cases, heading toward the altar as fast as they possibly could. He saw couples that did everything but intercourse. Mark most admired those who were choosing to hold themselves back. There seemed to be something noble, even heroic, about their efforts. It made his own relationships—he and Brenda had broken up, and he had a new girlfriend on campus where the same dynamics played out—look sloppy, he thought. At the same time,

Mark wasn't sure he could perceive a difference among all these couples and in the quality of their relationships. What made for a good relationship? There wasn't only one answer. Was it right to get married so that a person could have sex?

On Mark's campus, the Christian man's locker room wasn't a place where men bragged about conquest. They bragged about restraint. "She was really hot, but . . ." "She would've done it, but . . ." While it was a different sort of arrogance, it was still arrogance, and it was still sexually charged. It created an atmosphere of judgment and distance where vulnerability and truth seemed ephemeral. There were nights when Mark walked across campus alone and wished for an encounter with God that might "stand beyond words." He had worked so hard to do the right things. Where would God meet him? He felt like he was looking up into a cold and empty sky.

By the time Mark graduated, many of his friends were in serious relationships, engaged, if not married. Mark was none of these. But at the age of twenty-one, this didn't particularly bother him. He still had plenty of time to find the right person to marry and plenty of goals beyond marriage. As much as he had wanted to please people, he also didn't mind standing apart. He liked to challenge expectations, wrestle with questions, and make people think about things they took for granted.

The summer after college, he took an internship in the city. There, Mark met Lisa. Lisa was different than any other woman he had dated. Her mother was Jewish and her father was a Catholic, now agnostic. She didn't find the religious questions that perplexed Mark particularly interesting. She wasn't concerned with salvation or about a personal relationship with God in the same way he was. But

Mark was attracted to her incredible passion for goodness. She had worked for an orphanage in Mexico; she didn't eat meat out of a love for animals and a protest against the meat production industry, about which she knew a lot. She was planning on going to law school after she spent a year with an NGO doing relief work. Lisa's integrity, her engagement and absorption with moral questions, and her sharp mind and willingness to wrestle with questions outside of Mark's usual framework intrigued him.

Lisa and Mark went for walks. They sat in the park or took an outdoor table at a café and stayed there for hours talking. She invited Mark to parties with her friends who talked about books, politics, movies, and music all night. Mark and Lisa started to date, even though they were both leaving at the end of the summer. But they quickly ran into the problem of sex. Lisa perceived sex—sexual touching as well as intercourse—as a normal part of a relationship between people who cared about each other. Her perception of that did not seem conflicted or fraught, as far as Mark could tell. It just was. She didn't apologize for having sexual desires or for acting on them. She didn't have the reflex for repentance that Mark had internalized. The slippery slope felt more slippery with Lisa than it ever had with a Christian girl.

Mark observed people that summer who were breaking all of the rules he had received. They were living together, sleeping together, hooking up, breaking up. Yet all of them were, in a certain sense at least, good people. They had strong moral commitments and deep thoughts. They weren't shallow or callous or crude, at least not most of them. They'd read widely and thought a great deal about their choices. What did it mean in this environment to live as an authentic Christian? Mark often felt prudish, dogmatic, and judgmental. The foundations of his beliefs weren't as clear to him as he had thought, and his convictions seemed to come out more in recitation than in deep understanding. He struggled to make a meaningful translation.

The pull of his previous community was likewise strong. He had painful conversations with friends about Lisa. "Where does she go to church?" someone would inevitably ask. "She doesn't." Silence. He wanted to say, "Just because she doesn't go to church doesn't make her a bad person." But he knew how hollow that would sound. He didn't want anyone to think he was "missionary dating," dating someone he hoped to convert, but he didn't know how to justify his relationship with Lisa.

Mark's habit of keeping himself apart caused Lisa real pain. It was difficult to understand how a practice that was meant to bring about good could create harm. While respectful, Lisa was not striving to keep his worldview intact. When they were intimate, she did not help him police the boundaries; that task was his own. When he doubled down on his will, she felt hurt and rejected. Because of their myriad conversations about sex and morality, pride also began to play a role. Mark had said that he was committed to saving the most intimate acts of sexuality. His integrity was at stake. But Lisa took his distance to mean that he didn't really like her, so she also withdrew. Mark's "I have to hold myself to a higher standard" became to Lisa, "He thinks I have low standards."

Mark lived with a crowd of observers, mostly in his head, ready to judge his behavior at any moment. His parents, Aaron, professors at college, Christian friends, some of the people in his church, and various younger, harsher versions of himself seemed to have formed a sort of committee in his head, bent on policing his behavior with loving but stern intentions for his own good. Sometimes their voices were so loud, he could hardly hear himself think. In the circle where Mark came of age, he could say, "Sex outside of marriage is selfish. Withholding myself is a benefit to both you and me. Our relationship with God is far more important than our relationship with each other." That made perfect sense, and his inner committee roared with approval. But with Lisa, those words rang hollow. The translation was a failure. But still, if he had sex with Lisa, where would he then draw the boundary? They were both leaving at the end of the summer. There was little chance that the relationship would continue. How could he live with himself if he had what essentially amounted to a summer fling?

They did break up before the summer was over. Lisa cited their very different worldviews and wondered how they could be reconciled. Mark was, in a way, heartbroken, but decidedly changed. He'd been forced to see the world through someone else's eyes. The boundary between Christian and non-Christian, good people and bad people had dissolved, or at least been renegotiated. With that boundary gone, others were likely to transform as well.

During the first semester of his master's degree program at Indiana University, Mark met Angela. Again, her background challenged him. She was raised Catholic and had one very devout sister who was a mentor to her. She felt her own faith to be shakier than her sister's, but she admired her sister's passion. In high school, Angela had had sex with a boyfriend, but when that relationship ended in heartbreak, Angela vowed that she would wait to have sex again until marriage. Mark and Angela were both struggling with their respective traditions; they were both questioning and growing, and with her, Mark felt the deepest connection with a woman he had ever experienced. Since they shared the common ground of not wanting to have sex, Mark found himself back on the familiar continuum with her. They kissed, they touched, they felt themselves on the deliciously slippery slope. They both wanted and didn't want to stop. Mark's habits were the same, but his questions were changing. Lisa had exposed a weakness in his ethical foundation, so it seemed to him. He couldn't answer convincingly to himself the question of why sex was limited to marriage. What were the higher values that limitation expressed? Patriarchy? That's what Lisa had called it. Control of women's bodies for the sake of reproduction? Lisa had been relentless in her critique. Mark still believed that faithful marriage was the best form of expression of one's sexuality. Commitment, love, fidelity were all higher values. But with Angela, the "kissing-hugging-holding hands" triumvirate was giving way to a "love-trust-commitment" dynamic. Could sex be a beautiful expression of these qualities in a relationship? He could imagine Aaron's disappointment at this worldly turn. Nonsense. The Bible guards sex as belonging only to marriage. He had been taught what was right. Why was he now trying to invent a new standard? Lust? A secular ideology? Weakness?

Mark and Angela continued to date for two years until she graduated from college and went to Guatemala for the summer. Mark made arrangements to visit her. Their relationship was in flux. Angela was moving on while he still had at least a year left of his graduate program. She was younger and ready to travel. Should they break up or stay together, trying to make it work from a distance? The future was very difficult to see.

But when Mark arrived in Guatemala and saw Angela in her new environment, he was overwhelmed with love for her. She was beautiful, graceful, humble, kind, strong. He wanted to be with her forever, he thought. This time, when they started touching, they didn't stop. They had sex, even with none of their questions answered.

The next morning, Mark woke up early and walked around the streets of the foreign city alone. He walked past vendors pulling their carts to the market and watched women slapping tortillas onto griddles in the alleyways. The world seemed wider and more vivid than it had before. But he also noticed that he didn't feel that different; he didn't feel less like himself. He had created or had entered a world too far away to hear the committee. He had found a small voice to speak for himself, for his own experience. And maybe he and Angela had found a language of mutual love and mutual tenderness. It seemed possible at least.

Having sex didn't solve anything or really change anything. The voices in his head regrouped. Angela was still young and uncertain about her plans. Mark had his mind on school. They broke up a few months after Mark's return to Indiana. At the same time, Mark reflects, "I was forced to rethink what it meant to be moral and sexual with another person, a person just as complex as I am, filled with dreams and desires, bodies and beliefs. I was not giving up the quest for morality, but I also was not able to rely on that clear standard—even if it were to be held to again—and that pushed me more deeply into questions of goodness, what it meant to live relationally authentically in all the forms that relationships take, sexual and otherwise."

He could go in Aaron's direction of self-condemnation.

He could tell the story of Angela as one of sin and error. He could repent and regain his familiar footing. But something about that felt wrong, even self-indulgent. It felt petty and insulting to Angela, whose struggles he knew so well. On the other hand, was he ready to abandon the boundaries entirely? Scrap the life he had led for twenty-five years and start over? What alternatives were there?

Mark returned to his ordinary life. He studied, he ran, he went to church and helped lead music. But he gradually, quietly withdrew from Young Life leadership, no longer sure he could or should be the role model, especially when it hinged on a very specific sexual ethic. The party line didn't suit him so much anymore, if it ever had, but what was replacing it was only slowly emerging.

"I find my imagination," Mark said, "so undercultivated that I have a hard time imagining what form a new understanding might take."

For now, Mark is turning to poetry, art, music, and literature in an attempt to cultivate his imagination and find new ways through the wilderness. He is also learning to live on the margins of a worldview that was once his own center.

Megan

Megan thinks of her sexual story as beginning at the age of twelve. She fell in love with a boy who went to her church, a small nondenominational church in Kansas. At the moment that she and the boy noticed each other, her family was preparing to leave Kansas for Oregon. Before she left, the boy passed her a note asking if she would be his best friend forever, circle yes or no. She circled yes. Then he passed her a note asking if she would be his girlfriend. They kissed for the first time the night before she left for Oregon.

Her religious story begins long before she has any memories of it. Both sides of her family were deeply religious and went back generations on the same land and in the same community. Christianity was linked with home, family, stability, goodness, and farming. After her parents moved to Oregon, they struggled. Her mother talked about Kansas as if they were in exile from the Promised Land. In Oregon, the whole family seemed more adrift. Her parents moved from one church to another, complaining about the pastor there and the youth group there and the music someplace else.

They made several trips a year back to Kansas, and when they did, Megan saw the boy that she had kissed. Every time she went there, they kissed again. In between they wrote letters to each other. They frequently broke up in their letters and at the end of visits. They told each other they had to "live their own lives." But when they met up again, they started where they left off, and something about their absence from each other made everything feel both less dangerous and more exciting. They kissed and then went a little farther, touching each other, "making out," and then breaking up again.

When Megan's parents finally settled on a church in Oregon, they did so because of the youth group. They desperately wanted their kids to be involved in church, and they worried especially about Megan's older brother. They didn't think he had the genuine commitment to Christ that he should. He often clashed with her father at the dinner table, missed his curfew, and was, to say the least, a grumpy presence at church on Sunday.

Megan tried to make up for him. She cheerfully went to youth group, and it wasn't a chore. They played games—treasure hunts, lock-ins, trips to the water park, baseball in the summer, ping-pong and foosball in the church basement in the winter. The youth leaders were young and friendly. They led Bible studies and avoided topics that might make the youth uncomfortable, like sex. Megan gleaned the basics: sex is made by God for a man and woman to enjoy in marriage. Sex does not belong outside of marriage. The consequences of having sex outside of marriage are dire. She could see, to some degree, how this related to the boy back home. They had crept closer and closer to the line of "going too far," a state that was vague in their minds, but frightening. Pleasure and guilt accompanied her thoughts about him. She bragged about him to her friends in Oregon, and she always looked forward, almost desperately, to seeing him. But when she did, nothing was ever the same. She felt rejected and angry. She broke up with him; he broke up with her. It went on and on.

By the time Megan was a sophomore in high school, her brother's difficulties seemed to take over the family. The atmosphere at home was one of constant tension. One night, her father had to bail him out of jail. Her mother and father argued behind closed doors. Her mother was a nervous wreck almost all the time. Megan knew who he hung out with at school. She knew the kinds of things they did, and her parents were always plying her with questions about his activities, while he was always swearing her to secrecy. Megan felt divided and alone.

Gradually, she formed three very different Megans for three different contexts. At home, she was quiet and responsible, the kid her parents didn't have to worry about. At church, she was social and friendly, a youth group regular who knew the right answers to questions. But at school, she was a loner, shy and scared. She started slowly to make friends with kids around the margins, others who did not seem to belong. One afternoon, a girl from school invited her to come to her house after school. Megan accepted, and at Tara's house, she was offered a joint. She took it, and after smoking with Tara, she felt good, like she could forget everything. She started going to Tara's after school often. Smoking pot seemed like a way to get back at her parents for all the attention they lavished on her brother. She wondered how long it would take them to notice.

One day at Tara's, she noticed that Tara was staring at her in a funny way. "What?" she said finally.

"I wonder if you could ever have feelings for me."

"What kind of feelings?"

"You know, like, sexual feelings."

"What are you talking about?"

Tara told her that she was bisexual and that she found Megan attractive. Megan told her she didn't know if she could have those kinds of feelings for a girl. But she did go back to Tara's house again.

"Would you like to know what it feels like to be kissed by a girl?" Tara asked her, and before she could answer, Tara kissed her.

"I responded in that moment really intensely," Megan remembers. "My thought was, 'I am not supposed to be doing this, but here we go.'"

The relationship did not last long, and it ended in what Megan calls "typical high school drama" with screaming, slamming doors, and hanging up on each other. But it opened a door in Megan that she didn't know how to understand. She could feel romantically and sexually for both boys and girls. That fact surprised her, and she knew it was a secret of the highest order. Her parents would be beyond horrified. Her church would reject her. She would be an outcast.

Through the rest of high school, Megan kept the secret. She went to youth group, and she also went to parties, where she got high and had sexual encounters with both boys and girls. She did not "have sex," which she defined as intercourse. "Technically," she remained a virgin. She thought of her sexual encounters as similar to smoking pot. "I'm not choosing to do what is right."

The key issue for Megan became the double life she was leading: good church girl or wild party girl depending on where she was. She decided that duplicity would end with high school. When she got to the small, conservative Christian college that her parents were so delighted that she chose, she told her resident assistant almost immediately about the drugs and the sex. She told her that she intended to start a new life. She wanted to change. Her RA said that she should focus on her prayer life, and they would pray together.

Megan spent a lot of her first year in college focused on what she considered necessary healing. She wanted to "clean up" her mind and the intense sexual fantasies that had taken root there. She tried to look at people in new ways instead of just sizing up how "cute" or "hot" they were. Eventually, she decided to tell her parents about the sexual encounters she had had with girls. She decided that she needed to come clean and confess, so that she could reclaim her integrity and get on the right path. They were, as she had anticipated, horrified. "My mom asked me if it was because she hadn't loved me enough." Megan admitted that there was a grain of truth in that. "I didn't feel affirmed by my mother. She is overbearing and guilt-ridden, and she doesn't stand up to my dad. Not a female role model for me. So I looked around for what I wasn't getting from her."

Though the decision to talk to her parents was painful, all of the changes Megan was making were positive. She felt stronger and more whole after these conversations. But she felt helpless to change her attraction to women. That seemed to be the bargain that she was supposed to strike. If she became an integrated and honest person, then God would lift the burden of her attraction to women. She would become like everyone else. The only words she had for this attraction were *bad* and *wrong*. She gladly would have accepted these words and applied them to herself if that would have helped her to be rid of the feelings. But blaming herself seemed as impotent as her fervent prayers to God for transformation. As Megan got older, her sexual energy flowed more and more to women, and she could not stop it.

The way that Megan knew her desire was wrong was subtle. No one stood up and said exactly, "A sexual relationship with a woman is wrong." Instead the wrongness was conveyed through disgust that other girls expressed at the thought, through the relentless modeling of Christian marriage as the central goal of any girl's existence, through the pity expressed about those poor lost souls who wandered around outside of God's ordained truth.

At her college, there seemed to be a "Good Girls Club," and most girls were desperate to find their golden ticket and enter the club once and for all. They would do anything, say anything, be anything, if it would just confirm that they had finally been accepted into the Club. Good Girls talked endlessly about marriage. They knew exactly what their lives were supposed to look like, and they were working hard to shape them accordingly. Boys, romance, and the visualization of "someday" played important roles. Already, girls were coming back from the summer married and living off campus in apartments with their new husbands. These girls seemed to have won some prize in a lottery. Being married set them apart and gave them special status. They made everyone else seem childish, like they had lost a turn in the game of life. None of this game appealed to Megan, although she gave it a shot. She tried to study boys in her classes for which one would make a good life partner for her. She tried to suppress feelings for women and keep herself on the straight and narrow. But the truth was she didn't care much for the intense atmosphere of romance-leading-to-marriage. It didn't suit her, and she found it shallow.

When prayers to change didn't have any effect, Megan

tried abstinence. She could just keep her body and her feelings to herself, she decided. But that didn't work well either. She was not adept at the skill of friendship. Megan would become quickly attached to girls that she wanted as friends, and then get angry and hurt when they didn't give her all of the attention she wanted. She was emotionally dependent and found herself spending a lot of time pouting.

After a couple of years of these cyclical thoughts and feelings, Megan introduced a new thought. Maybe her sexual feelings for women wouldn't go away because they weren't "bad" and "wrong." Maybe God didn't answer her prayer to change them because they didn't need to be changed. Maybe it was possible to have a relationship with a woman that had all the goodness a heterosexual relationship was supposed to have. This thought didn't come from her environment, at least not directly. She knew it was a form of heresy. Women's sexuality was derived from male sexuality. It was a direct result of being desired, chosen, by a man. The goal of female life was to be in a relationship with a man, and until that relationship unfolded and seemed on a path toward marriage, all sexual desire and sexual feelings were illegitimate and unacceptable. Sexual feelings between two women fell far outside "God's plan" as Megan had learned it since she was small.

Once a year, the campus held an event called "Let's Talk About Sex" that was for women only. Preparations for the event started months in advance. A small committee selected candidates for a panel and met weekly with those candidates in preparation through the fall. In the weeks leading up to the event, posters went up all over campus in sexy and dramatic colors like pink, red, and black. The edginess and difficulty of discussing sex was obvious in how hard everyone worked to pull off this event.

Megan was involved in the planning and organizing. She took up the responsibility to handle music for the worship segment, but she was careful not to reveal any part of her own story—especially her attraction to women. At the event, seven hundred young women gathered inside the chapel and sat on the floor. Organizers had tried, despite the large size, to create an atmosphere of intimacy. They dimmed the lights, lit candles, and played soft music. On the walls, they put words that were normally not spoken, but that here would be safe to say, words like *clitoris*, *orgasm*, and *masturbation*.

For the first half hour, Megan led the auditorium full of women in a worship service that was mostly music. She'd selected songs that were prayerful and contemplative, introspective and soothing. She invited the young women to respond to the music physically as well as emotionally. She suggested that people could move, sway, or dance to the music if they wanted to. Only a few did. Most sat in quiet, either out of fear or in an attempt to pray—or both.

Then the panelists who were lined up onstage each had about two minutes to tell their carefully scripted stories. Organizers had tried to select a group of women with diverse experiences. Some were simply young women who had already married. Others represented various kinds of forbidden sexual experience. There was the "masturbation" panelist and the "I got pregnant in high school and had an abortion" panelist. There were panelists who had never held hands with a boy and now were scared that they would never have sexual feelings. No one, anywhere, at any time, mentioned the possibility of women's desire for other women. "If they had mentioned that," Megan said. "They would have had to acknowledge that it existed and even had to enter into the debate about whether it was OK or not

OK. By not acknowledging it, they didn't have to answer hard questions." Megan herself slipped a question into the pile for the panelists about homosexual desire. Organizers quietly ignored it.

The atmosphere was confessional. The purpose of the panelists—even of the sessions leading up to the event—was to tell their deepest, darkest secrets, and to talk about sin and redemption. Any sexual experiences that fell outside the bounds of already prescribed rules had to be told by a formula: the woman had to confess: "I gave my boyfriend oral sex in high school." And then she had to describe the impact of the sin: "It made me feel bad and dirty inside." Finally, she had to say that she was no longer behaving in that way: "God really changed my heart, and I know that I am forgiven." If the panelist was a married woman and therefore had a legitimate claim to sexuality, her message often was: sex is harder and more disappointing than you might think, especially the first time.

In some ways "Let's Talk About Sex" was the culminating ritual of the Good Girls Club, a way that those who had fallen outside the lines could be welcomed back in and those who remained inside could feel secure. They could appear to have addressed the complicated and taboo topic of sexuality, while not acknowledging much of its complexity. While there were stories of error, there were few gray areas. The panelists felt it was their responsibility to answer questions, not raise them, and there was little room for individuals to have different stories or, as one observer put it, "different depths."

After the panelists had spoken in an atmosphere of hushed and reverential respect, the young women had an opportunity to ask questions. They could either submit the questions anonymously or stand up to ask them. Organizers selected the handwritten questions and handed them to the panelists. The questions focused repeatedly on the same theme. The only thing about sex that the girls seemed desperate to know was this: What is OK and what is not OK? Is it OK to masturbate? How far is too far with touching? Which parts are OK to touch? "I let my boyfriend touch my breasts, and then we broke up and I feel devastated. What should I do?" And so on. The lines that the girls were so desperate to find had to be iterated over and over again, and yet somehow, no iteration was satisfying. Somehow the boundaries did not hold.

After the event, organizers were careful to make sure that the girls had somewhere to go—other events scheduled. In part this was because they were concerned about how the subject of sexuality can touch such raw and deep emotions, and they wanted to be sure that the girls had a safe place to express themselves. On the other hand, Megan thinks, another purpose was to make sure that the theologically correct positions stayed theologically correct. There was to be no room for rethinking or for questioning. If the girls had questions that had not been asked in the room, then they should be directed to appropriate resources. And perhaps a third reason, the least acknowledged of all, was that the atmosphere and the topic were arousing. The body had been invited in. The senses had been titillated. Who knew where that would lead? Better to be sure to channel the young women to safe activities than send them out, charged, into the world.

Megan had mixed feelings about her participation. On the one hand, she was clear that her own story would not be welcome in that atmosphere. Even if she were willing to tell it in a confessional mode, which she wasn't, she wouldn't be welcome to. On the other hand, she liked the topic and the provocation it caused. She liked the way it seemed to change the conversation and raise real doubts. Frankly, she loved the sensuality of the atmosphere. For her, it was a turn-on.

One thing that no one knew was that she had met someone, and this time, she could tell, it was different. Instead of diving in emotionally and creating drama, as had been Megan's pattern, she and the girl, Lily, took their time getting to know each other. As their friendship developed, gradually, so did their physical relationship. At first, they just did what Megan calls "aggressive cuddling." They held hands, then they held each other, then, eventually, they kissed, all the time trying to talk about it openly.

Maybe, Megan thought, sexual touch was beautiful, even sacred. A little crack appeared through the familiar wall of guilt and shame. But not easily. Lily was younger than Megan and had never been in a relationship with anyone. They vowed to stop touching each other until they were ready to commit, but they both struggled with what that meant, and they didn't have any models around them to follow.

Not wanting to be secretive, Megan and Lily "confessed" their relationship to their roommates, after they had vowed to stop touching. They asked their roommates to "hold them accountable." But that too felt wrong, as if they were groping in the dark toward a doorway and finding it locked. They knew that the only legitimate way to talk about their relationship was to confess it as something bad. They had to regret it and be trying hard to change. They had to ask other people to hold them accountable to this change, even when they weren't sure they wanted that accountability. So when Megan and Lily wanted to establish integrity, to make their relationship visible, the only way they could do this was through confession and repentance. If they talked about their relationship but refused to repent, that was tantamount to heresy. They could be expelled from school, and even if not, they would certainly be shunned.

🐝

In this, Megan's senior year, all of the girls were reading a book called *Captivating: Unveiling the Mystery of a Woman's Soul* by John and Stasi Eldredge. A copy sat on Megan's roommate's desk. Megan picked it up one day and read the first few pages. She heard that a "Captivating Retreat" was coming up on campus, and that everyone was excited about it. She was curious what the hype was about, although she made sure that she was scheduled to lead music in church that week so that she couldn't attend.

The book claimed to be laying out a new path for male and female Christianhood. In the introduction, Stasi expressed her dismay at the current literature for Christian women. It piled an incredible list of "shoulds" on women; it claimed to know just exactly how hard a woman needed to work to please both God and her husband. It reinforced the message that a woman is not enough just as she is.

As an alternative, the Eldredges claimed access to the true desire of a woman's heart. They claimed to cut through all the guilt to reveal women's true natures. Elements of this sounded good to Megan on the surface, but she was suspicious that the Eldredges would have any insight into her true nature. The true nature of a man, the Eldredges taught, was to be a "warrior" with a "wild heart" who takes an active part in the grand adventure of life, especially in pursuit or protection of his "beauty"—a woman. Women's true nature was exactly complementary to this. A woman longed "to be romanced, to play an irreplaceable role in a great adventure, and to unveil beauty." "Come now," wrote Stasi in one of many rhetorical questions. "Wouldn't you want to ride through the Scottish highlands with a man like Mel Gibson?"

"Not really," Megan thought.

Megan couldn't help but notice the passive verbs—a woman's job is to be something to and for a man; to follow his lead; to join his adventure rather than have her own. This book was irrelevant to the challenge Megan was facing, yet everyone around her was reading it as if it contained some great secret they had been waiting all their lives to learn. That was *the* way God made women to be. Why did she not feel that God had made her this way? The book raised the question she had been asking for years: am I defective?

At the Captivating Retreat, the other girls reported, the women had been invited to identify lies they had accepted as myths about themselves. "I am not enough. I am not lovely. I am not important. I am too needy." Megan felt surrounded by people who had accepted lies about themselves and called them truth. She thought about her mother. Had her mother ever asked about her "true nature"? It seemed to Megan that her mother had done what she was told, followed all the rules, and ended up unhappy. Megan felt like her mother had been whispering to her all along, "Don't go the way I did," but she couldn't guide her to another path.

Megan felt that she, too, had accepted lies about herself. Chief among them was that if she just worked hard enough on herself, she could change. But there, Megan's ability to hear the Eldredges' message stopped. The next part of the lesson taught at the retreat was that women needed to cultivate a truly "feminine heart" and find their true desires, which were essentially men.

"It doesn't seem right," Megan said. "To be waiting around for a man to fulfill you."

"What do you want in a guy?" her hallmates never seemed to tire of asking.

When Megan and Lily had told their roommates about their relationship, one of them had said, "I just can't wait for you to meet the guy you are going to marry." That comment, with all of its insensitivity and insipidness, seared Megan to the core.

There was, however, another aspect of the *Captivating* philosophy that did appeal to Megan: romance. She was embarrassed to admit it, but she thought about romance all of the time. She dreamed of making Lily feel utterly special, chosen, and loved. Cherished. One of her friends had told her about a boy that she had been friends with for years. One night, he staged a treasure hunt and a picnic supper and asked her to be his girlfriend. Megan loved that story and went over the details in her mind. She didn't, as *Captivating* would have it, imagine herself romanced. She imagined doing the romancing. She wanted to stage a moment like that for Lily. In her fantasy, the moment was a mix of both the intimate and the public. There would be no more secrets, no more hiding, no more pretending. She would offer her private feelings and her passion to Lily, but she would have those feelings publicly acknowledged. She loved to go over the details in her mind, even as she and Lily were keeping their distance and remaining "just friends."

Sex remained a source of confusion and hope. Her best, deepest, most meaningful relationships had come out of friendships, and she wanted more of that. "Love," she reasons, "has to do with being in a place of truth with another person. When that place of truth coincides with deep intimacy on all kinds of levels . . . it is almost a way to worship God, to be close with God. The true meaning of sexuality is vibrating on the same chord with another person."

The spirituality of her sexuality was only just beginning to dawn on her. Megan went to a "welcoming and affirming service" at the local Episcopal cathedral. It was an evening communion service. At the service, Megan and another friend looked around at all the beautiful people gathered there. For the first time, in the space of a church, she felt utterly and completely accepted. She felt the tenderness of her failings and of those around her. She sensed the immense mercy of God. Megan also heard a message that she felt profoundly: yes, we are gay, lesbian, and transgender people. Yes, our path is different from others, and we are often excluded and rejected. This does not excuse us from doing the hard work of God in the world. We are not allowed to wallow in self-pity or dwell on our stories. We are meant, just like every believer, to be at work in the world, preparing to make a difference, to demonstrate the love of God for all. Megan and her friend absorbed the intense, loving, gentle atmosphere of the service. When it came time for Eucharist, they each served it to one another. When, later, they went back to campus, they felt like they had found the door to Aladdin's Cave, like they held a tender and precious secret about God that they couldn't share yet with those around them.

Megan and Lily were not able to stay away from each other. The depths of their feelings and the strength of their attraction won out over their intentions. They decided that, in fact, they were in a relationship with each other. They were lovers. They would have to tell their friends and their families—not in order to confess and repent, but simply for the sake of their own integrity. To have these initial conversations, they went over and over their scripts. They had no models, and they didn't know what the right words would be. They rehearsed and they edited until they felt that they had something close to the right way to talk to their parents and their friends. Megan laughs remembering how seriously they took these "coming out" conversations. In every aspect of their relationship, they felt pressure to perform "the perfect lesbian Christian couple." She now thinks that there perhaps isn't a good or a bad way to come out. People will react the way they will react. All a person can do is be honest.

For Megan, this was very new territory. She was accepting a new sexual identity. She was allowing people to see her as a lesbian who was in a relationship with Lily. Her sexual desire was no longer a terrible secret, but something that made her visibly connected with another person. She and Lily now had the difficult work of figuring out how to be together. Again, there were no models, no rules. They were both devout Christians. They both wanted to keep their relationship with God intact. While their relationship put them at odds with their community, it also underlined their commitment to it.

In a heterosexual, Christian relationship, the rules—however often fudged and negotiated—have a certain flow. You can go to second base with someone if you've been dating a long time. If you are engaged, well, no one is going to say that everything but sex isn't OK. That's your own business and so on. These guideposts and milestones mark out a relationship and its boundaries.

But Lily and Megan had to invent these on their own. "We really worked on the theology of our relationship, on how to be together," Megan recalls. "Sexually, we went a lot faster because we didn't know the boundaries. We went a lot further than we might have if we had been in a het erosexual relationship, probably. Our invisibility gave us a kind of permission." At the same time, they also came to embrace an ethic with each other: presence. They learned that sexuality is about being with a whole person, respecting that whole person. If either one of them was scared or not fully present, then the other person's job was to respect that and offer comfort and safety.

Megan and Lily dated for three and half years. After graduation, they lived in separate apartments with separate roommates. They talked a lot about lifetime commitment and lifelong monogamy but were not willing to move in together. Each went through stages where she was ready to commit and then stages where she backed off. They did not know what a commitment would look like or how to make it. Again, they felt in a no-man's-land, without rules.

Then one day, Lily came back from a Bible study meeting with, she said sheepishly, a message for Megan. She handed Megan a piece of paper on which was written Jeremiah 13:11. "I don't know what it means," Lily said. "It just came to me while we were praying, and something told me it was for you." Megan went to look it up.

> "For as a belt is bound around a man's waist, so I bound the whole house of Israel and the whole house of Judah to me," declares the LORD, "to be my people for my renown and praise and honor. But they have not listened."

Megan's first response to having "received" this scripture was rage. "I have spent the last three and half years listening," she said to God. "I haven't been doing anything but listening. I have been asking you over and over again if this relationship is OK, if I can have this kind of relationship. I have told you that I am willing to give it up, if only you will bring me peace about it. So what is this supposed to mean?"

When her rage subsided, the revelation that lay behind it changed her. "You have been only listening to hear no," she heard God say. "I have been trying to tell you so many things besides no. I gave you this relationship. It has brought nothing but goodness to your life. Are you listening to the answer yes? Are you listening to the reality that I love you and I want to love you this way?"

Megan and Lily broke up only recently. Megan had begun to have doubts that they would ever commit to each other permanently. Lily also had begun to have doubts that she was ready to make that commitment. Megan was the only romantic interest that Lily had ever had. For a long time, their doubts went unspoken, and then Megan did something that she says she will regret the rest of her life: she spent the night with another woman. It had begun as a harmless flirtation and developed into something that Megan had not even acknowledged in herself that she intended to pursue. And yet she did.

Soon after that, Lily and Megan broke up, and the next several months were nightmarish for her. Megan drank too much and found old habits that she was disappointed were easy for her to fall back into. She felt unlovable and unloved. Gradually, she is beginning to find her feet again, to walk out in the world, taking all of her history with her as she goes, and giving thanks for each moment of it, as best she can.

Part Two

Incarnation

Sarah, Mark, and Megan, as well as many others of us, have spent significant time in what I've called the wilderness, where religious faith and sexuality do not find an easy relationship, where confusion and uncertainty mar the landscape and the way forward is not clear. But in a way that should not surprise us—wilderness is also a place where God meets us and whispers new possibilities and coaxes us into a bigger world, full of more grace than our worlds held before. Our tradition tells and retells this story. Moses, Abraham and Sarah, Hagar, the Israelites, Elijah, David, and Jesus all go to the wilderness, and in the midst of confusion, fear, danger, and uncertainty, they find God's presence and a path to a greater understanding. The wilderness cannot—like the Apostle Paul says of death, life, angels, principalities, height, depth, present, future, or any other power—separate us from the love of God. At the same time, the wilderness offers no easy answers.

The Christian tradition offers more than the wilderness from which to draw resources for the integration of sexuality and faith. Another crucial aspect is incarnation. One of my first acknowledgments of the possibility of incarnation came in college during a modern dance class. I was not a dancer, but I decided to take the first section of modern dance as many times as I could before graduation. I did not intend to move on to Modern Dance II. That was too ambitious. But in Modern Dance I, the professor would ask us to lie on the floor. Then she would say, "I want you to move from your kidneys." I had no idea what she was talking about. It was baffling. I lay on the floor bemused by my inability to fathom what she meant. "Find your center," she would say. Physically, I had no idea how to locate it.

I came to modern dance over and over again precisely for this reason: I didn't really know anything about my body. I fed it what the diet books said I should (information that was becoming increasingly baroque and contradictory). I did with it what I was taught I should, but I didn't have a relationship with it. One of the problems that led me to modern dance was that I lacked the physical confidence to walk across a room. I'd spent many an evening trapped in the back corner of a party because I could not muster the courage to stand up and walk across the room to the door. To do so was to risk being seen. Being seen meant being physically present, occupying space, becoming real to myself.

Very gradually, I learned embodiment. This is the process that is an important part of what I am calling incarnation, and I live in a culture that is miserable at it. Instead of learning from the sensory world, we aim to control it. We put ourselves on diets to control rampant eating, but we are pitiful at tasting. We make budgets to control rampant consumerism, but we know very little about actual pleasure. As a whole, our society grows heavier and more debt ridden with each passing year. If control of bodies were enough, if books about the right way to do things could transform us, then the $40-billion diet industry would be bankrupt.

In his book *Techgnosis*, Erik Davis describes the intersection of technology and spirituality that can make our physical presence in the sensory world less "real" to us than our digital presence. Gnosticism was an early Christian teaching that was eventually expelled from Christian orthodoxy. Gnostics, in the early days, argued that Jesus only appeared to have become human, but in reality, he was never made of the same stuff that we are. Gnostics were suspicious of the claim that God substance could become human substance. They were scandalized by the thought that Jesus might actually have died on the cross. Gnosticism came from the Greek word for *knowledge*, and Gnostics believed that they had special insight into the spiritual realm.

In the first-century Middle East, Gnosticism had resonance for women and people who were in the underclass. "You" were your body, and if that body was female or enslaved, then you were trapped by that physical circumstance. Many women were attracted to Gnosticism because it promised that, on a spiritual level, women could become men. That idea was attractive because it meant access to a new kind of freedom. If Christ's body wasn't physically real, maybe there was a spiritual way that we could become like Christ, and that would wipe out all-determining gender and class difference. To transcend one's bodily fate was deliverance.

We, on the other hand, live in a very different world. We do not necessarily see ourselves as our bodies. Our "true self" might be something very different from our bodies, even encumbered by our bodies. Our bodies are medicalized, dissectible, diagnosable, objectifiable, and ultimately transcendable. In our wired world, bodiless transactions take place all the time. I "see" and "speak" with people I never meet. For us, reclaiming the body as central to who we are, investing in our own incarnation as central to our faith, could be an important step in integrating sexuality and faith.

When I first starting working on this book, I was speaking with a college chaplain about the problem that many of her students were having with online dating relationships. Many young women, and at her college it appeared to be a problem mostly associated with women, were getting sexually involved with men they "met" on the Internet. They might never have physically met these men, but they spent hours and hours absorbed with them online. Their grades, friendships, and overall health were suffering because of the time they spent having virtual sex with strangers. The chaplain was struggling with how to intervene.

While this is by no means a problem unique to Christian colleges and Christian girls, we do know that American Christian culture is weak on incarnation, and that this may contribute to the particular theological problem these girls developed. When my priest calls us to the altar for the Eucharist, we stand in a circle, and she offers us bread and wine. She sometimes tries to remind us to be alert to God's presence in this here and now, in this time and this place, with these particular people. The time to try to embody the love of God is now.

The priest at my Episcopal church feels the need for a better grasp of incarnation with particular urgency because when she was a young woman, she was anorexic. The desire to starve herself into nonbeing was a powerful urge that had many layers. One of these layers was the desire for perfect control over her body and herself so that she would have no impact on the world around her. She would be invisible and thus make no mistakes. At a certain point, the realization became clear: she would soon "perfect" herself out of existence. If she did not stop, she would die. She decided not to die, but then she had the painful task of becoming flesh again. She remembers the first moment when she had put on enough weight to feel the skin of her upper arm touch the skin of her rib cage. The sensation terrified her—flesh touching flesh, her own flesh touching her own flesh. But if she wanted to become alive like Hezekiah, if she wanted to "live and not die," she had to allow herself to become flesh. Standing now at the altar welcoming people to the Eucharist, she urges us to accept our incarnation—enfleshment—as the heart of our faith, as goodness.

Theologically, incarnation is tricky. Is Jesus's incarnation like ours? Or is it different? For some Christian thinkers, the key to understanding Christ's incarnation is sin. Christ took on our sinful natures, and we should be glad that he lowered himself into our dirty bodies. His incarnation is nothing like ours because he is God and we are not.

While this might be the most common interpretation in American Christianity, it isn't the only one available in the Christian tradition. For Orthodox Christians, *Logos* is not only the Word of God dwelling in a single human form, but also in the "totality of human nature, in mankind as a whole, in creation as a whole," as theologian Philip Sherrard describes it. In other words, Jesus became incarnate in the body of one person and in the totality of all creation. The Eastern Church describes Jesus as fulfilling a promise present at the beginning of creation and continually present—the promise of God's presence with us. Even if, early Christian writers said, we had never sinned, Christ would still have come to fulfill that promise, out of love.

This idea has taken many forms through Christian tradition. In the twentieth century, Jesuit priest and philosopher Pierre Teilhard de Chardin suggested that Christ is a "fire with the power to penetrate all things" and that the Incarnation should be understood as an ongoing and ever-present reality deep in the "heart of matter." In the fourteenth century, visionary Julian of Norwich insisted that "we are in Christ, and Christ, whom we do not see, is in us." I do not think that Julian, whose theology of incarnation was intricate, meant that Christ dwells in some abstract place called the "soul," although she did imagine a dwelling place for Christ there. She struggled to understand the connection between what she called our "sensuality" and God's "substance." At root, she saw that sensuality and substance were united in Christ, and in us. In ancient times, the idea of Christ's incarnation overcame the divide between heaven and earth. The idea that God might take human form was a scandal. In our day, the idea that God might dwell in the physical body is a scandal. There is still a similar divide to overcome.

Perhaps incarnation is not best understood in systematic theology or even recited in creeds. Perhaps the best access we have is through poems, stories, songs, music, and art. In contemporary poet Christian Wiman's poems, I sometimes gain a glimpse of incarnation. In one poem from his most recent collection, *Every Riven Thing*, the poet sees birds resting in a winter tree. For a moment, the birds are just birds—flesh and bone and feather. The tree is a seemingly dead, gnarly thing. Then in an instant, and for just a moment, he glimpses another way to look at the birds and the tree. The birds take flight, and the poet experiences an inexplicable and irretrievable moment of joy. The world is not only what it appears to be. The tree and the birds both transcend themselves, and he is able to see that there is a surprising and holy connection between himself, the tree, the birds, and a kind of divine, enlivening presence.

Incarnation is like that connective tissue. It is an integrative word, a word that takes scattered pieces and joins them, unifies them, and points toward the possibility that they are always, already unified. The Sufi master Moussa Tine mixes dirt into his paint because, he says, "soil and light" are the key elements of his holy work.

Christianity seems capable of expressing this truth. Journalist and recent convert Sara Miles writes that she was drawn to Christianity because of "the compelling story of incarnation in its grungiest details, the promise that words and flesh were deeply, deeply connected."

We have to press forward for a vocabulary that can express the intertwining of flesh and spirit. This will be crucial in taking up Mark's call to expand our imaginations. But American Christians have a long way to go to grasp incarnation, as I think these next three stories aptly demonstrate. Because we live in such an airy reality, we compensate by making a large number of rules about the body: dietary rules, sexual rules, religious rules, exercise, seat belts, health, wealth. Everyone who knows me well knows that I love rules. I am always making new ones. My head is such a thicket of rules that I have almost reached the point where I cannot tell which one I am following at any given moment. I read diet magazines and fitness advice. I devour the latest material on health to see what new rules I might add. I read spiritual self-help books and writing advice manuals.

But perhaps, I (and we) can begin to see our way forward, out of the thicket of rules, with the premise that our bodies are holy. I do not mean this in the sense of "your body is a temple of the Holy Spirit" so you'd better keep it pure or else. By contrast, I mean that our bodies are already enlivened by the presence of God; they are already singing, as the French philosopher Hélène Cixous says, "unheard songs." They are, already, a means to know and love God. We don't have to buy anything, practice anything, or believe anything to make it so. We just have to breathe in and out. We experience God every time we breathe. That's how tenacious the love of God is.

To say this is not to say that our bodies do no wrong. That there is no sin in the world. That we are never wronged and never do harm. We know that our experience, our bodies, our lives are marred and wounded by sin. But we can still say, paradoxically with Julian of Norwich, that "sin is nothing" in comparison with love. Each of the people in the following three stories has come by embodied knowledge through pain. Each points the way toward a deeper understanding of our own incarnation, and so of Christ's.

Monica

The first time Monica saw a woman's naked body that was not her own and not in a movie, she was studying life drawing. When the session of drawing nudes was announced, Monica felt an inexplicable wave of anxiety, as if she herself were going to pose nude and not be safely seated behind a desk in a room with a dozen other students. In thinking about the first session, she expected that she would find the model beautiful, so she tried to minimize her anxiety by looking at it as an exercise in aesthetic appreciation, like painting water lilies or mountain landscapes. In her mind, model plus naked plus woman had to equal beautiful, otherwise why do it? But she had little foundation for this belief.

When the day came, she sat behind her drawing table with her pencil and sketch pad. The model came out and seated herself. Monica felt a wave of repulsion. The woman serving as a model for this drawing was nothing that she had expected. She was, for one thing, fleshy. You could see pockets of cellulite on her thighs and collected fat at the tops of her arms and at her hips. Under the lights, you could see places where she had missed shaving. She was human, a human body, and that not only surprised Monica; it made her nauseous. The words that came to her mind embarrassed her: revolting, ugly, disgusting. She could hardly endure the session as the professor laid out the assignments and expectations and as students began their first sketches. She repressed a desire to flee, but after class, she studied the schedule wondering if she could get out of this.

Walking back to her dormitory, Monica asked herself why there was such a difference between what she had expected and what she had seen. The first time she had seen a naked woman had probably been in some forbidden R-rated movie when she was growing up, something she might have watched with her cousin in his basement. The idea was that you got a fleeting glance at the woman, not an up-close and personal look. There was no time to study the woman's body, just enough to say that sex, nakedness, and beauty all went together. It was exciting in part because it was forbidden. They hoped their parents wouldn't walk in just at that part in the movie. Another time one of her cousins had shown her some magazines with naked pictures that he had hidden out behind the barn. She'd felt excited, terrified, sick. But again, these pictures and the model in the art class had little in common.

In other words, without realizing it, Monica had formed her entire idea of the human body, her own body, from secret, "dirty," fleeting images, from forbidden places and forbidden contexts. This more recent and more extended exposure under the fluorescent lights of the art studio was something entirely new, entirely different, and extremely uncomfortable.

Monica's life-drawing class was taking place during a semester abroad. Monica encountered the model literally thousands of miles away from her family and her home, from the ranch in northern Idaho where she had grown up and the conservative Christian college where she had just spent two years. The distance allowed her to contemplate what to do. She decided to face her fears and go back to the class.

❦

Monica grew up in a close-knit, almost clanlike family. Her parents lived on a ranch with her grandparents, uncles, aunts, and cousins all close by. She was an only child, and she spent many of her early years on the ranch with her grandfather, doing chores and roaming the tall grasses and small forests of the land her family owned. She and her grandfather built birdhouses together, and she romped through the wet grass to hang them on fence posts.

Religiously, her family was almost reflexively conservative. The Baptist church they attended was rural and had had the same families as members for decades. You could almost name the pews after the people who sat in them week after week. Her family had a prominent place in the church. When she looked around on Sunday, she could name every person and their connection to her family. The family was ruled, patriarch-style, by her grandfather who took a significant role in "training" the children of the family. Her parents, by comparison, were obedient, almost passive, and they let her grandfather dictate family life, for good and for ill. Her parents' faith seemed anemic when compared with her grandfather's, as if it had been watered down with the change in generation.

Sexuality was not something anyone talked about. When Monica was six and a schoolmate told her how babies were made, Monica simply said, "No way." It was an utterly unimaginable reality. Yet within a year of that conversation, an older cousin led her into an upstairs bedroom, pulled down her panties, and touched her "down there." She felt wrong about it, although she couldn't explain why, and he insisted that they keep it a secret. In some ways, she liked receiving special attention. Her parents were not affectionate, and sometimes she felt invisible in the world.

At the same time, her cousin's touch gave her a queasy feeling, and she came to associate that feeling with everything sexual. It was nothing if not confusing.

Equally confusing and terrifying was the adults' reaction when they found out. Her cousin's mother screamed and cried, whipping herself into a frightening hysteria. Monica's mother settled her mouth into a straight line and said nothing at all except, "Don't do that again," though Monica didn't know what she had done. Neither of them ever spoke about it, but it stayed there all the time, a wordless monster. None of this had helped explain what had happened. She had said no to her cousin many times, and that hadn't mattered. Then she felt that her mother blamed her and did not care to listen to Monica's story. How she felt about anything appeared to be of no consequence. Her parents and her grandfather treated her as a possession. The older she got, the more choices were made for her, in the name of keeping her "safe," although she never felt safe, not even in the presence of those whose job it was to guard her.

When Monica was twelve years old, two things happened that seemed to signal two very different claims on her body, two very different paths for her life. One was that her parents and grandparents decided that her days of free roaming on the ranch had best be over. Her grandfather announced that it was time for her to learn proper women's work. She was given the task of cooking and cleaning the house, with little instruction. Her own mother worked in town as a receptionist at a dentist office and was not around to teach her. When she came home from work, her mother would slap her and scold her for things not done properly, as if that would teach her the right way.

Other than that, her parents came home from work

and turned on the television. Her mother said that evening dramas were "too secular," so her parents watched the Trinity Broadcast Network, the evening news, *The People's Court*, and even soap operas that they taped during the day. The TV seemed to take her parents away to a place still farther from Monica, and she felt always alone.

At the same time, another thing happened when Monica was twelve that seemed utterly different: she was baptized. She prayed to "give her life to Christ" as she had been taught to do and then prepared for baptism. To prepare, Monica had written out her testimony, a record of why she had come to believe in Jesus as her Savior and why she had accepted him into her heart. On the day of the baptism, she walked out into the center of the baptismal tank and read her testimony nervously and quickly while the water soaked the white robe she wore. Then she set the paper on the side of the tank. She pinched her nostrils with one hand and held that wrist with the other hand, as she had rehearsed with the pastor. He stood next to her in the water, his suit pants wet to his thighs, a microphone clipped to his collar. With one hand on her back and the other on her clasped arms, he tilted her back into the water. "I baptize you in the name of Jesus," he said. In her mind's eye, she can see parts of the baptism that she wasn't physically able to see at the time. She imagines herself suspended in the water, the blue-green of the tank, the thick white fabric of the robe swirling, her hair briefly hovering over her face. She feels the warmth of the water over her whole body.

"What if my sins really are washed away?" she thought. She could taste freedom in that possibility.

The baptism was over in a moment. The pastor raised her from the water. She climbed out of the tank, went out a side door and down a flight of stairs where there were dry clothes and a hair dryer waiting for her.

The God of baptism was a God who made her feel safe, a "refuge" like the psalm said. She felt cared for, forgiven, "hidden in the shadow of a rock." He had a purpose for her, she believed that passionately. She clung to it.

Her parents sent her to a Christian school, again with her safety in mind. The school believed in values-based instruction and "character development." Character development seemed to come mostly in the form of shame and silence. People could be expelled for kissing in the hallway. Once a friend leaned over to her during an assembly and said, "Which boy do you like?" Before Monica could respond, a teacher interrupted them, "We don't talk that way here, girls!" Somehow, from listening to other kids and paying attention, Monica came to think of herself as good but not pretty. Pretty girls had boys like them no matter what the school said about it. At best, she perceived, she could hope to find a Christian husband who would overlook her shortcomings for the sake of her strong faith. The message she heard from every corner was: you do not belong to yourself. You are not your own. You belong to us and you will do what we say.

Monica's only form of rebellion was a deeply private one, silent and secret: masturbation. She knew that touching herself was wrong and that other people would say she was bad for doing it. Perhaps as a consequence, her sexual fantasies were often violent. She imagined being tied up, raped, even beaten by her "lover," punished for being ugly, punished for needing love.

After contemplating what course of action to take, Monica returned to the drawing studio for one reason: she admired the woman's courage and wanted to honor it. Monica felt she owed the woman, who was a lot braver than she was, some respect. "What was beautiful anyway?" Monica wondered. Why was she so sure that this woman wasn't beautiful? How did she know?

Monica went to class and practiced sketching. Since she was so far from home, from the Four Square Gospel church where she went in her college town, from her family, she allowed herself to experiment. No one was going to report her. No one would tell her parents. Part of the mystery is that the other students didn't seem to find this a dirty, secret thing. She didn't hear anyone at the coffee shop after class say, "Did you see that model? Wasn't she repulsive?" Monica kept her judgments to herself. The other students thought she was a little odd anyway, lacking in sophistication and a bit naively religious. One good thing about growing up in her house was that Monica knew how to keep her mouth shut.

Monica had not gone to college intending to study art, although everyone had always said that she was good at drawing. She thought she might like to study biology. On the other hand, the thought that she was special, that she might have some special vocation had stayed with her since she was young. "They" said her special talent was art, so she signed up for art classes as well as biology classes and soon found herself absorbed in art. She found that art had a way of drawing her closer to God. Her brain and body worked together to form a prayer, and prayer was the only way that she could make art. As she silenced the multitude of inner voices, she used her hands to speak directly to God, and God seemed to answer, also through her hands. Art became an important means of communication with the God who had always whispered to her of love and freedom.

She decided to participate in the life-drawing class as a form of prayer. She asked God to teach her as He so often had through art. It took a long time. Gradually, she began to notice the way that the woman's shoulder connected to her neck. That was beautiful. A luxurious curve. She practiced drawing that curve over and over. Her hand moved with the motion until she and the curve were aligned. The first sketches were just that: neck and shoulder with a bit of profile and a bit of arm. As she drew that part of the woman over and over, she grew to love it. The motion of her drawing stayed with her even when she was not in class. She started to crave going back to try again.

The shoulder and the neck led her to think about how other parts of the body were connected. What about the hip and thigh? The shoulder and the arm? The knee and the shin? These interstices, meeting points, were how the body was made. From a drawing point of view, that was fascinating. An artist could never finish exploring these connections. When Monica thought of how the body was made, the words of Psalm 139 eventually came to her:

> For it was you who formed my inward parts;
> you knit me together in my mother's womb.
> I praise you, for I am fearfully and wonderfully made.
> Wonderful are your works;
> that I know very well.

Fearfully and wonderfully made. Fearfully—that part she understood better than she liked. Wonderfully—that part was still mysterious but increasingly evident. She could see the truth in both parts, and she could even try to capture that truth with her pencil.

Another phrase came to her while she was drawing.

It was from one of her theology classes at college: *Imago Dei*. The image of God. We are made in the image of God. Until now, she hadn't any idea what that meant. She'd never thought of the image of God as something physical. She remembered that her professor had said that the biblical writers would probably have had something physical in mind, but that was hard to grasp. In what sense were we, physical beings, made in the image of an immaterial God? How was that possible? In drawing, she could give her wondering an immediate application. She would ask as she drew what it meant that this woman was made in the image of God. She could draw her *as if* she were made in the image of God.

The next significant thought came after some weeks of drawing. The thought came to her as if it were speaking to her from the outside and whispering in her ear. "You are made this same way. I knit you together like this. You are fearfully and wonderfully made."

When Monica returned to college in the United States the next semester, she knew that something in her had changed. She was less self-protective, more open with her friends. She was less afraid of everyday interactions. In a way she couldn't quite grasp, this was tied to the drawing.

That fall, when she was a senior, the chair of the department invited her to hang her art in the library. She didn't give a second thought as to what to display. Her best work was the work she had done while she was abroad: the sketches of the nude model. She framed the sketches on simple white mattes with narrow black frames. As she arranged the sketches on the wall, she thought about how she might help the viewer enter in slowly to see what she had seen. Then she placed a comment book on a small table with a pen and stepped back to look at the sketches. She felt a flood of love for them and for the woman who had dared to teach her.

For all the care that Monica had taken in her preparations, she had forgotten one thing: the opening of her show coincided with parents' weekend at the college. There was a firestorm of response:

"Why did you put these disgusting pictures in the library?"

"Go take your pornography someplace else."

"This is an utterly inappropriate display for a Christian college."

Someone complained to the dean, who called the chair of the art department for a conversation. But, in the end, the sketches remained on the wall of the library.

Monica heard two things in the comments. She heard the same fear and revulsion that she had experienced in herself when first encountering the model. It was a disgust that humans exist in this form—as if the people who were looking at the sketches had been able to avoid that knowledge until her pictures confronted them with it. She also heard in the comments that Christianity and nakedness were incompatible—somehow being clothed and being Christian were necessary to each other. By now, her study of art had progressed far enough that she did not take this assumption for granted. She had seen many paintings of the naked breasts of Mary—paintings that conveyed somehow to people of another time and place that God cared for them and fed them. She had seen many a naked Jesus as well, conveying through his body—often torn, bleeding, too thin—the vulnerability and simplicity of his humanness. Christians had used the nakedness of Jesus to say, "He was like us." Nakedness hadn't always conveyed pornography to Christians.

The sketches did not only spark negative comments—although it was the negative comments that stung Monica. Some people wrote, "Thank you for your courage." Others commented on the way that she seemed to handle the female form with remarkable love and honor. Another wrote starkly, "I was raped. I see in these drawings my self-worth."

In art classes, Monica had studied the difference between "nude" and "naked." "Nude" seemed closer to the expression of devotion that she had intended. "Nude" connoted to her the respectful distance, even awe, as opposed to the exploitative demand for exposure. "Nude" suggested that a body could be cast in an almost holy light. At the same time, that word had been used for centuries by mostly male artists to impose on female models the idea of perfection. Perfect proportions had been debated by artists and art historians for centuries. Kenneth Clark was a twentieth-century art critic who articulated this position well. He called the body of the model in its naked form "shapeless and pitiful." "We do not wish to imitate," he wrote. "We wish to perfect . . . We are immediately disturbed by wrinkles, pouches, and other small imperfections." He went on to say that the models should be painted to conform to the ideals of the artist's time, "which should be the kind of shape which men like to see." The thought made her physically ill, even inexplicably enraged.

"Nude," in that sense, meant that artists changed women's bodies to accommodate their perception of female ideals, instead of receiving women as they were. So in this way, she was not inclined to see herself in that tradition. It wasn't perfection that she wanted to understand; it was incarnation.

Incarnation, she thought, was something like God's

desire to know us. It's one thing to create and another to know. When she first started to create sketches of the model, she hadn't really known her. But as she began to connect the sketches of this stranger to her own being, that action changed the way that she lived in her own body and the way that she created art. When Jesus—God's Word—took human form, wouldn't he also have wanted to know us? Would he have longed for intimacy and knowledge, like she did? Incarnation was a physical form of knowledge—a knowing with the body—that could only come from living.

That spring, she called her senior show *Passing Away*, as in 2 Corinthians 5: "So if anyone is in Christ, there is a new creation: everything old has passed away; see, everything has become new!" The show was a series of self-portraits—herself nude. She tried, awkwardly at first, to extend to herself the tenderness that she had extended via her pencil to the model in the art studio. She also began to ask friends to model for her, and she took up a camera so that she could play with light and dark in these photos. She even asked a male friend to model, wondering if her camera could convey the same expression of honor to his body. The answer was no. She was too afraid of him, and her fear overtook the art, but she filed that information away for another time.

Meanwhile, another idea had occurred to her, another way that she could continue to wonder through art: she drove into downtown Portland and volunteered herself to be a nude model at a community art studio. She felt that, at last, she was ready to be the Imago Dei for others. She didn't do it because she thought herself perfect, but because she knew she could be present. She could bring incarnation to others as it had been brought to her.

Paul

When Paul arrived at the second parish that he served as pastor, he found a figurine of Christ shoved at the back of the pencil drawer of his desk. He yanked it free from where it had been stuck and pulled it out. It was a heavy pewter figurine of Jesus, twisted in agony.

He carried it out to the secretary. "What's this?" he asked.

"Oh, that's the body of Christ from the processional cross. One of the church people brought it back from Rome. Where did you find it?"

"At the back of the pencil drawer."

The secretary smiled. "The previous pastor thought it was too Catholic, so he unscrewed it from the cross."

Paul studied the image of Christ in his hands. He thought of the Apostle Paul's words, "We preach Christ crucified." He thought of how many times in his life he'd run from those words.

"Where's the toolbox?" His first job at his new church, he later joked, was to screw the body of Christ back on the cross. Three screws: two for the hands and one for the feet.

"People would prefer to have inherited a more disembodied religion than Christianity," Paul says. "But this bloody Jesus is what we've got. Like it or not."

Paul took a long path to embracing this reality for himself. Grasping the significance of the Body of Christ had not come easily to him.

One of the songs that Paul sang as a choirboy in his Lutheran church in northern Iowa was "A Mighty Fortress Is Our God," the classic Lutheran hymn written by Luther himself. It could be belted out with full force, and Paul had always thrilled at the unifying voices at the chorus, as if together their voices were creating the fortress.

> A mighty fortress is our God
> A bulwark never failing
> Our helper he amid the flood
> Of mortal ills prevailing.

Inside the walls of the church, Paul imagined being safe. Paul loved everything about the church—the candles, the processions, the robes, the heavy metalwork of the sacred objects. He considered himself a "dutiful son." "That really defined my identity in my family and in the church," Paul says.

The choir loft was adjacent to the altar in Paul's church, and from there he had a good view of the pastor: his rich vestments in changing colors, the way he lifted his arms at the Te Deum. Facing away from the congregation, he sang, "We worship you. We give you thanks," as the sleeves of his cassock waved.

The music of the church and its liturgy was home—a place of warmth, stability, and comfort. It was almost a secret, separate world. Every Sunday had the flavor of a festival. Depending on the season, the church would be draped in purple, white, red, or green homemade banners. The pastor would dress in a flowing robe with matching stole.

The silver of the Eucharist chalice appeared at the hymn of thanksgiving. "This is the feast of victory for our God. For the lamb who was slain has come again," the choir sang.

The choir rehearsed in the sacristy where the children were allowed to sit on the kneelers for communion. The sacristy was the place where all the holy things were kept, and Paul loved to be among them and become a part of them. Paul loved the heavy polyester choir robes and their velvety hoods. When the choir director placed the hood on each child and led them out to the choir loft, Paul felt anointed.

In athletics and school, Paul was less sure of himself. He didn't feel he quite belonged. He wasn't competitive. He loved to be outside and wander the farm and the woods around his home, but he didn't enjoy sports. His friends came from church and from music, in which he excelled.

From a very young age, Paul felt vocationally set apart. He knew he was meant to be a minister. The church that Paul and his parents attended was part of the Augustana Synod of the Lutheran church, a group of Scandinavian immigrants with deep ethnic ties. Both his maternal uncle and his maternal grandfather were ministers. His grandfather would draw Paul aside, set him on his knee, and say, "Now, Paul, you want to be a minister, right?" It was a rhetorical question, but Paul did want to be a minister. He'd never wanted to be anything else.

In the second grade, the children were told to prepare a special presentation for parents' night at school. Each one was supposed to draw a picture of what they wanted to be when they grew up. Paul could see in his mind exactly what he wanted to draw. He could see the altar and behind it the cross. He could see himself dressed in cassock and surplice.

But the thought of actually drawing this picture embarrassed him terribly. He didn't like the idea of taking his secret world into the public. He drew himself as a park ranger instead. But that choice nagged at him. He felt anxious that his parents would go to the school, see that picture, and be upset. He decided to warn them, "I really *do* want to be a pastor," he said. "But it was easier to draw a tree." Even as a seven-year-old, he felt he had betrayed his vocation.

Paul's mother had a deep, even fiery, faith. In Paul's 1960s childhood, she was attracted to the charismatic movements that were influencing even the staid Lutherans of the Midwest. She was far too deeply Lutheran to ever leave her church, but she did want to see it "infused with the Holy Spirit." She was a follower of the dynamic evangelist Kathryn Kuhlman, who was famous for her healing services. Kuhlman was a tall, elegant redhead who dressed in flowing gowns and spoke, despite her Tennessee roots, with an Audrey Hepburn lilt. She was a powerful orator, who drew people of all denominations to her. She was condemned by the Pope for attracting too many Catholics to her movement and criticized by her fellow Pentecostals for being too soft on Catholics.

Paul's mother loved Kuhlman's weekly television show *I Believe in Miracles*, where the stately Kuhlman sat in a formal parlor and addressed her audience with a tattered Bible in her hands. She exuded both intimacy and authority, femininity and a powerful transcendent force. Her voice, when she preached, could be soft and refined or gritty and deep. Kuhlman held rallies in huge stadiums where people came from all over the world to be healed. Kuhlman exalted in her worldwide following, but she refused to be called a "faith healer." She was not responsible, she said, for the healings that had taken place. God was.

Paul traveled with his mother on late-night bus rides to charismatic conventions in the Minneapolis auditorium. Thousands of people came from all over the Midwest to experience the working power of the Holy Spirit. At one workshop, his mother, who had always suffered from severe back pain, said she experienced a heat coursing through her body. Though Paul has no idea how to interpret this event now, he admits that his mother never again complained about her back. She'd been healed, she said.

The charismatic movement offered Paul's mother an experiential element of faith that went beyond the "word and sacrament" of her traditional Lutheranism. Through Kuhlman and the Lutheran Conference on the Holy Spirit, she was drawn into the realm of signs and wonders. As in the words of the song "A Mighty Fortress" she claimed the "spirit and the gifts" for her own. This expressive religion unleashed the body into the realm of the spirit, drawing them close together in passionate and dramatic display. Her desire for this alternative was strong enough that she could overlook the whisperings about Kuhlman's sexual transgressions, financial misdealings, and grand accumulation of wealth.

In Paul's rural community where the smell of cow manure and pesticides blew in from the surrounding farms, Paul's mother and a group of like-minded Christians from several denominations felt that the church had been sleeping. In the midst of all the social and political turmoil of American life in the 1960s and 1970s, the church needed a wake-up call. Its power needed to be ignited. The intense pace of social change meant that these awakeners were open to the ideas of dispensationalism: the coming of the Rapture and the end of the world. Hal Lindsey's *The Late Great Planet Earth* struck Paul, in his early teen years, with urgency. Surely this was the final age. "I hope," he told his mother, "that I get to graduate from high school before the Rapture comes." In this atmosphere, it was hard for Paul to imagine a future for himself that wasn't connected to a rapid decline of the world. At a Lutheran camp, he sang, "I Wish We'd All Been Ready" around the campfire—a song about the danger of the coming tide and the terror of those who would be left behind.

At a youth group gathering, he watched *A Thief in the Night*, a movie about the Rapture, and wept during the scene when a pastor explains to his parish why he failed them and hadn't prepared them for the Rapture.

While charismatic Christianity might have offered Paul's mother an impassioned complement to her Lutheranism, the stew of dramatic and fearful Christianity wasn't as beneficial to Paul. He came to view all institutions, including his own little Lutheran church, as suspect. He and his friends were suspicious that their own pastor would be left behind in the Rapture, that he didn't really have the Holy Spirit.

"We were a thorn in the pastor's side," he recalls. "A real group of zealots." Paul was equally suspicious of other young people at Lutheran Youth Encounter retreats. He looked down on the more worldly kids, like the girl and boy caught together in a sleeping bag.

The world outside frightened him, and his fear forced him more deeply into his own head. At one Lutheran League convention, he and a friend gave a presentation on the dangers of rock music. They associated it with drug use and Satan worship. Popular music represented to Paul a dark and sinister youth culture he was determined to stay away from. He channeled all of his energy into being a good kid, a "child pastor," "everybody's best friend," and a good musician.

Paul and his friends found an alternative in the burgeoning Christian music industry. They listened to Keith Green, Amy Grant, and The Second Chapter of Acts. Paul was especially drawn to the sun-drenched world of Evie Tornquist. Evie shared with Paul a Norwegian heritage, and she had the sweet voice, deep dimples, and ethereal presence of an angel. Paul fell in love with her and wrote her letter after letter.

He and his friends developed a Bible study in which they scoured the Bible, especially the New Testament Epistles, for the right way to live in the End Times. "Flee from sexual immorality. All other sins a man commits outside of his body. But he who sins sexually sins against his own body. Do you not know that your body is a temple of the Holy Spirit who is in you, whom you have received from God?" These words deepened Paul's sense of himself as a fortress to be defended. Flee, Paul would.

At the same time, Paul spent his summers at the local swimming pool where he developed intense, wordless crushes on the pool's male lifeguards. These crushes were far more intensely physical than anything Paul felt for Evie, but they never became anything more than an unnamable longing. Other than stark warnings, sexuality was neither discussed nor acknowledged in church settings. Since, for Paul, everything that was a part of the church was real, and everything that was not part of the church had a sheen of unreality about it, Paul was able to suppress sexual impulses for a long time. "My spirituality," Paul says, "just overshadowed my sexuality. I always lived in my head and not my body. Everything having to do with sex was wrong and sinful. I was afraid of God, afraid of the consequences, afraid of addiction. The old adage, 'Once you start, you won't be able to stop.'" So Paul decided not to start; he imagined that part of himself could simply be screened off.

The Rapture did not come. Paul graduated from high school and attended a small Bible college not far from home. With the help of others, Paul managed to create a beautiful container from which the world could be observed, but not engaged. For better or for worse, the container had to be shattered. Upon graduation from college, two things happened almost simultaneously. Paul's father—a quiet, kind, stoic man—died suddenly of a heart attack, and Paul ended a relationship with a woman he had intended to marry. The final straw of their relationship was an argument about baptism. Paul was heading to a Lutheran seminary to become a Lutheran pastor. Lutheran pastors baptize babies. Paul's fiancée felt passionately that baptism must be a choice, not forced on anyone in infancy. They could not agree. Each remained entrenched in their position without a way forward. Paul left for seminary more alone in the world than he had ever been.

Paul was one of a very few seminary students who came to campus wearing Reagan buttons in 1984. As one of the most conservative students, he found himself constantly on the defensive. Seminary initially intensified his long-cultivated feeling that his faith existed in opposition to the forces of the world. In his second year, he found himself seated in the front row of Gerhard Forde's class "Creation and Redemption." He had been warned by many fundamentalist friends that seminary would be hazardous to his spiritual health. His mother was concerned about his faith at that "liberal" seminary. So he entered the class with his guard up.

Forde was a classical theologian with deep roots in the Midwestern Lutheranism shared by Paul's family. He was not a "liberal" theologian, but he was a passionate expositor of "radical grace." In the classroom, he was a formidable presence with a perfectly trimmed, professorial white bread and horn-rimmed glasses. His teaching was part lecture, part proclamation. A sober Norwegian, Forde rarely smiled, but frequently sprinkled his lectures with dry-humored jokes.

Paul was intimidated. Confronting a man of such passionate faith, so different from his own and yet so learned and from the same roots, was confusing. Using Paul's letter to the Romans and the writings of Martin Luther, Forde taught that we are freed by grace and that any and all "righteous action" begins from this freedom. Paul found himself dumbfounded. He had read Paul's letter to the Romans dozens of times, studied it in Bible studies and in college. But even though he was a traditional Lutheran, he had not really ever heard the teachings through the lens of grace. He sat with his head and heart burning, arguing viciously but silently with Forde. God wanted, no demanded, our righteousness. "Looking back, I am sure Forde could tell how angry I was, how uptight, how completely outside my body and myself. I am sure he knew exactly where I came from." But Paul was also ready to be changed. "In truth," Paul says, using a peculiarly Lutheran orientation to theology to frame his new understanding, "I was being put to death through the proclamation of grace in his teaching. The unconditional nature of God was obliterating my old systems of thought. I was being grasped by grace for the first time."

At the same time, Paul fell in love with a seminary classmate. He longed to be in the man's presence, loved the sound of his voice and the way that he brushed his hair off his forehead. He loved their conversations and the depth of understanding they seemed to reach effortlessly. When Paul fell in love, he had the thought, "So this is what they were talking about." It was the first time that the sensation—at once physical, mental, emotional, and spiritual—had been able to reach him. As grace took shape in Paul's understanding along with the feeling of being in love, he was at last able to speak the truth about himself to himself. The reason he had locked sexuality up in a tight box to which no one had access was because he was gay. If God offered us unconditional love, Paul said tentatively, experimentally, to himself, then God was not afraid for us to be who we really are.

But Paul reached this conclusion in his final year of seminary. The man with whom he had fallen in love was not himself gay. While he helped Paul grapple with his new reality, he wasn't able to fully share the dilemma. Meanwhile, all energy and attention settled on ordination. Paul's primary concern about his ordination—the fulfillment of his lifelong goal—was not his sexuality, but the possibility that he might not be Lutheran enough. His evangelical background, his now-waning charismatic leanings made him question his legitimacy as a Lutheran. The acknowledgment that Paul was a sexual being and that he was gay did strike him with an enormous wave of grief. But it was simply too big a fact to be grappled with in the intensity of the moment. He had to put it away for a while. He was used to having his sexuality locked up in a box. It could stay there while he pursued his vocation.

Paul was ordained and sent out to his first pastorate in a small town in southwestern Minnesota. Since in Paul's mind "gay" and "minister" would not fit together, Paul decided that he would just be celibate and single. He would not have relationships. He would not practice his homosexuality, in which case it would be nobody's business. "Dutiful son," Paul says of his first pastorate. "There was a part of me that always wanted to prove that I could be who they wanted me to be at any cost." And yet, that cost seemed to grow bigger during Paul's first year. A voice sometimes nagged at him: Did being a pastor mean that he was not supposed to be a whole person? Did it mean that he was supposed to be cut off from intimate love for his whole life?

After the first difficult year in a small church, Paul decided to go to Florida on vacation by himself. He wanted to use the vacation to peer into the small box that he now carried with him. The box said, "I am gay," but Paul really didn't know much more about it than that. Who was the gay Paul? How was he different from the asexual man that he had known all of his life? On vacation, he took two books. One was called *Come Home! Reclaiming Spirituality and Community as Gay Men and Lesbians*, by Presbyterian counselor Chris Glaser. The other was called *Half Laughing, Half Crying: Songs for Myself*, a collection of essays by gay Christian activist and celebrity Malcolm Boyd. On the beach in Florida, toes digging into the warm sand, in a beach chair surrounded by strangers, Paul read about himself. He filled the books' margins with notes of intense self-recognition. Like Boyd, he found himself half laughing at the startling clarity and half crying for all that his new reality meant.

Glaser wrote about the gift that gay people could be to the church because of the way that sexuality and spirituality were forced to come together in a deeply embodied way. "Sexuality is a means of grace," Glaser wrote, so that we may know how intimately God loves us. He wrote that God had made people gay "in the womb," as part of their formation, and so God would not abandon them now. He wrote that integrity demanded that embodiment, that gay men and lesbians could overcome the pain of their exclusion and "come home." Paul did not feel that the church had excluded him—he had not really given it that opportunity. But he did feel that he had excluded an enormous part of himself, shunned it. That shunning of himself was just as painful as any other exclusion, and it had to end. Paul wept as he understood that while he had intended to give the church himself—at whatever cost—he was actually denying the institution that he loved his whole self. He was burying his talent out of fear.

When Paul returned from Florida, he knew that he couldn't stay in this tiny pastorate with all the new knowledge that he had. To do so would simply be to cut himself off from himself, and that no longer seemed viable. Paul began to look for ways out—ways that he could serve the church he loved and become a more complete human being. He imagined himself planted at this parish for his whole life and withering from lack of love. The thought pained him terribly. Just as music had been his first path into the church, he decided that music was a way out.

He applied for a PhD program in sacred music at Yale University. As a church musician, without the particular burden of the pastorate, Paul felt that he could begin to explore what it meant to be gay. Maybe—at thirty years old—he could go out on dates. Maybe he could fall in love. Maybe he could learn something about this body that he had been given. He turned in his resignation and drove away from the pastorate in what he called his "getaway vehicle," a 1993 gold Suzuki Samurai with a "ragtop and a roll bar." He arrived in Connecticut to find a way to be free of the burdens of his lifelong calling.

❧

At the time when Paul was wrestling with his own identity, the question of ordination for gays and lesbians in the
Evangelical Lutheran Church in America (ELCA) had yet
to reach its fever pitch. The tacit agreement between the
denomination and its pastors was something like the mili-
tary's "don't ask, don't tell" policy. Gay people could serve
as clergy, of course, as they always have, as long as they
were not "practicing" and were not in relationships. It was
a harsh and unexamined policy that in essence demanded
the disembodiment that Paul had known all of his life. But
it also seemed perfectly reasonable, because it absolved the
church from having to deal with the too-painful question
of gay relationships and the reality that gay people had no
legitimate way to be sexual and stay in the church. The
assumption among most gay people who had grown up
in the church was that there was no reason for them to
stay. The assumption among most church people was that
there was no reason to ask them to stay, and if they chose
to, they should keep quiet and play by the rules.

These assumptions were on the precipice of a radical
shift. Gay and lesbian clergy of the ELCA were beginning
to build what they initially called the Extraordinary Can-
didacy Project where gay and lesbian people who felt called
to ministry could get support and help. This developed
into a roster of "extraordinary clergy"—people who would
not be accepted into the ELCA officially, but who had all
of the skills and vocation of non-gay clergy. Eventually,
this organization would challenge the broader church's assumptions and break the silence.

But Paul was unaware of this as he went to Yale and
pursued his other extraordinary passion: music. He never
thought of leaving the church. It would be like cutting off

his limbs. But he was determined to find a way to serve it while keeping himself intact. Being a pastor did not seem to fit these criteria.

On January 24, 1993, Paul was driving home from a church music assignment in New Hampshire when the Suzuki slid on black ice. He turned upside down on the side of the road, his car landing between two boulders. "Either one of the two boulders would have killed me," he remembers. "And I landed between them." An older couple pulled up alongside the accident, and he heard the woman's voice, "Dear God, let him be alive." He was alive. In fact, the accident awakened him dramatically. He walked away from the accident with only a "single drop of blood on his finger." The next day in chapel was the feast day of the conversion of Saint Paul. He identified profoundly with the apostle's roadside conversion. "It came blasting through that day that my call was to integrate everything: my gay self, my pastor self, my good boy self." Like his first-century namesake, Paul was not going to be allowed the luxury of running away.

Still Paul did not go back to his pastoral identity easily and swiftly—that integration from that moment forward was not simple. He finished his degree and applied for parish ministry in Malcolm Boyd's hometown. This time he arrived to an urban parish in California where he found the body of Christ in the drawer. He had taken himself out of the drawer, like that body, and he was ready to screw himself back onto the pastorate, whatever that meant. But this time, he was determined to do it as a full human being.

More than a decade later, Paul was serving as pastor at another church in California when he decided that he had not yet done enough to reconcile his homosexuality and his church. After moving to California, Paul had fallen in love with a man and had been in a relationship with him for several years. At the church he served, Paul's sexual identity was not an issue. His bishop did not see any purpose in his exclusion and the people of the church were accepting. At the same time, he had been tentative about bringing his relationship forward. True to his Scandinavian heritage, he just didn't bring it up.

After much wrestling with the idea, Paul decided to "come out" at a church-wide assembly in Florida. Church members and clergy were invited to speak on proposals before the church council on sexuality. Paul added his voice to dozens of others, both for and against various resolutions. But Paul decided not to speak about his positions on issues. He decided simply to give the "issue" of homosexual clergy a face, a name, and a body. "I am a third-generation pastor of this church, a gay man, in a relationship of profound love and commitment with my beloved partner of eight years," he said.

The response that Paul received was mostly silent, with some encouragement sprinkled in. Returning home and returning to work, Paul wondered what was ahead. The church was in turmoil, and the issue of whether homosexuals should be "allowed" to be clergy was paramount. It seemed odd to Paul that a pocket of peace surrounded him. Paul didn't know why he had not faced the intense rejection that so many other gays and lesbians experienced in the church. He didn't know why he never had a conflict with a bishop or faced exile. But when the time came, he was able to use that place of relative comfort to speak for others.

The time came a few years later when the question of "extraordinary clergy" had reached a pinnacle. A pastor at a large, dynamic church in the southeast had been serving a church for several years. When he started at the church, he had gone to his bishop and said, "I am gay, but I am not in a relationship. I thought you should know." His bishop had said, "I see no reason to do anything about this now. If you ever are in a relationship, let me know, and we will figure out what to do." A few years later, the pastor fell in love with a man and went back to his bishop with the information that he was now in a committed relationship. His bishop turned him over to the synod for prosecution. The church itself refused to let him go. They decided they would rather have an "illegal" pastor than give up the pastor who had served them so well.

Paul saw that he had an important opportunity. He offered to go to the trial and be called as a witness. But when he arrived, he was told that the prosecution did not want him to take the stand. After several days of wrangling, the prosecution agreed that Paul could submit his testimony in writing. "It makes sense, you know," one friend said. "The church wishes gay people would hide, so they take the words from your mouth." For a Lutheran minister, the connection between truth and speech is intimate. The written word is not the same as a word proclaimed. "Faith comes by hearing," Paul explains. "We need to be freed by an external word. That's because we are knit together, and we are being known by each other. That is redemption."

Paul returned to California disappointed. His friend lost the trial but continued to serve the church. But in his own church, Paul had found at once his voice and his body. He knows what his work is. "People are waiting to be freed. I want to liberate them. It really is OK to be in your body. They have an eager longing to hear a word that gives freedom. What I say to people now is: how can a greater body part say to the lesser body part, we don't need you? We all make up the body, and all the parts are honored. If we believe that, then where does the judgment come from? I say to people, which part are you? The asshole? But what would you do without it? Even the most queer body parts are important. That's what I try to lift up in community."

Ashley

The music pounded in Ashley's headphones as she completed her set of lat pull-downs at the gym. She listened to the Christian rock group Caedmon's Call, and especially to their song "This World," often during her workouts because she believed that the music helped her stand strong. Their words were about the abandonment of all the world's demands. There was nothing, she believed, in "this world" that was of value. Her goal was to be strong in body, mind, and spirit. To stand in purity and righteousness against an oversexualized, hedonistic culture that was intent on corrupting young people and leading them on destructive paths.

The music, on the other hand, emphasized spirituality, morality, and a path of righteousness, the desire to be closer to God. Above all, the lyrics emphasized transcendence, transcendence over the body and everything else that was of "this world."

Transcendence was now nineteen-year-old Ashley's watchword, her guiding principle. She longed for it and tried to practice it in body, mind, and spirit. To live by God's rules and to become less like oneself and more like Christ, to be perfect as her heavenly Father is perfect: these were Ashley's goals, and she lived them every day. What she did not know, what was a secret still hidden in her toned and muscled body, was that as she became skilled at transcendence, she was very close to dying.

Ashley begins her story at an earlier moment, a few years before this workout in the college gym. She was raised in a small city in Colorado and grew up in a conservative German Lutheran church. She attended Sunday school and participated in church life with her mother, a talented church musician, and her father, an elder. Ashley was active in the church youth group but not yet fully committed to Christianity when she had her first boyfriend. His name was Ryan, and they played together in the school orchestra and walked home together after rehearsal. Ryan was funny and sweet, but after they kissed for the first time, Ryan's interest in her waned quickly. She felt embarrassed and ashamed. What had she done to turn him off?

Her second boyfriend, Cody, was a swimmer. Perhaps he got Ashley's attention because he was so unlike Ryan. He wanted to be with her all the time. He was jealous of anyone else she talked to and wanted to know what she said to her girlfriends when he wasn't there. When Ashley came home from a date with him at the movies, she noticed that she had bruises on her wrists from how tightly he held her hand. He never felt like he got enough of her attention. One day, she had agreed to attend his swim meet, but for reasons she no longer remembers, she arrived late. Just as she walked into the pool area, Cody was getting out of the water after his race. She had missed it. When he saw her, his face darkened with fury. He crossed the room, dripping wet, and before she could speak, slapped her across the face and punched her on the arm. She remembers nothing else—not whether other people at the pool responded or how she left or whether she told her parents what had happened. But at that moment, she quietly decided that she had to put an end to this relationship. It wasn't easy, and it took a few months to finally extricate herself, but eventually Cody found another girl about whose attention he could obsess.

After these two miserable, early attempts at relationships, Ashley heard a message loud and clear that had begun to circulate in her church youth group: dating was bad and dangerous to a person's spiritual health. That message resonated with Ashley.

The time was the late 1990s. In 1993, an evangelical pastor, Joshua McDowell, had formed an organization in Nashville called True Love Waits. Its intent was to counter the culture of promiscuity marketed to teenagers by the mainstream media and to lead a movement of sexual purity and abstinence. McDowell encouraged teenagers to sign abstinence pledges stating, "Believing that true love waits, I make a commitment to God, my family, my friends, my future mate, and my future children to a lifetime of purity including sexual abstinence from this day until the day I enter a biblical marriage relationship." Just as significant as the pledge itself was the "purity ring" that many girls donned as a symbol of their pledge.

By 1994, True Love Waits had developed an effective campaign that had spread nationwide and made the cover of *Life* magazine. A photo in the magazine showed a youth rally where 211,000 teens had signed pledge cards and stacked them to the ceiling of the stadium. Over the next decade, True Love Waits and many similar organizations sold bumper stickers, T-shirts, posters, and jewelry—all using consumer culture to sell this alternative message. Joshua McDowell traveled the country telling teens that sex should be saved for marriage only. But he was not interested only in sexual intercourse. His message included control of sexual thoughts, masturbation, kissing, touching, and any other activity that could threaten the purity of a Christian young person.

In 1997, Joshua Harris took McDowell's message one step further. He published a book that had a dramatic impact on Ashley's young life. In *I Kissed Dating Goodbye*, Harris writes that the rules about sexual behavior are not enough. He advocates that young people commit to not dating one another at all. "As I see it, dating is a product of our entertainment-driven, disposable everything American culture," he writes. Instead of dating, young people should commit themselves to friendships, their relationship with God, and service to others. Dating should be saved for a time when a person is truly ready for marriage.

For Harris, purity is of central importance. Purity is not only about who or what touches the physical body. Harris insists that "God wants us all to pursue purity and blamelessness in our motives, our minds, and our emotions." In the book's opening example, Harris imagines a wedding that turns into a nightmare. As a young man stands at the altar, all of his former girlfriends come forward one at a time to claim a piece of him. He had "given a piece of his heart to all of them" and therefore did not have a whole heart to give to his bride. In this conception, purity is a finite, all-too-easily expendable quantity. Pieces of the heart cannot be reclaimed. "God knows," Harris warns, "that we will carry the memories of our physical involvements into marriage" and live unquestionably with doubt and regret.

The message Harris sent to women includes the age-

old idea that women cause men to sin. Maybe they can't
help it, but they could always do a better job trying to pre-
vent it. Harris urges women to cover up their bodies so as
not to make allowances for sinful thoughts and to be good
at policing the boundaries so their male counterparts aren't
tempted. Young men are offered the rather virile job of
becoming "warriors" for the purity of their friends who are
girls. They are charged with guarding the purity of other
men's future wives.

"True purity flees as fast and as far as it can from sin
and compromise," Harris writes. Purity is a zero sum game
where human experiences and relationships are contami-
nants. Life does not teach; it sullies. Ambivalence is weakness. Either a person lives a godly life or they know no
limits.

Ashley learned very well the rules of no compromise.
After reading *I Kissed Dating Goodbye*, she carried an arm-
load of tank tops from her closet downstairs to where her
mother was playing the piano in the living room. "I don't
want these anymore," she said. "From now on I am going to
dress modestly. I don't want guys looking at me and thinking impure thoughts."

Her mother looked at her quizzically. Then she said,
"Take those right back upstairs and put them in your closet
where they belong."

Ever obedient, Ashley took the tank tops upstairs and
shoved them to the back of her closet. They symbolized
the plan she had for her burgeoning sexuality: conceal it,
put it away, and leave it alone. The seeds had been planted.
A pure life was a life-denying one. Desire had no limits, so
one must suppress it as completely as possible or become a
slave to it. No compromise.

After that, Ashley started dressing in men's clothing. On her thin body, she put her father's oversized work shirts, and she wore baggy pants that she rolled up at the bottom. Her message to herself and to the world was clear: her body was not safe. In baggy clothes, she sought a degree of safety. "It wasn't a butch thing for me," Ashley recalls. "I just wanted to cover up my body as much as possible." No one would look at her as an object of desire.

Ashley was extremely good at putting her goals into practice. While many teenagers might simply go through a "Joshua Harris" phase and then go on to experiment with other ways of living out their values, Ashley kept the new rules she made for herself vigorously. She didn't allow herself so much as a crush on a boy. She dated no one and allowed no one to touch her. She studied the Bible and attended hundreds of youth group functions. Along the way, something else also happened gradually, almost imperceptibly. Ashley stopped eating.

An active teenager, busy with school, music, work, and church, Ashley didn't have time for meals. She was worried about both her mother and her sister, and for some reason, felt charged with taking care of them. She would put loads of laundry in the washer and pack a lunch for her sister, without ever thinking of her own food. Her parents, deeply absorbed in their own lives, rarely put meals on the table or policed anyone else's food. They rarely sat down together at the table for dinner, and her mother was always trying out a new diet. When Ashley got through the day eating only a few hundred calories, no one noticed.

Ashley finds it difficult to say which came first: not eating or the theology of not eating. The theology of not eating went like this: our society is sick from rampant desire. To come into relationship with God, He demands that we control our bodies and our desires. Ultimately, our only desire should be for God. Food is one key place where lack of control can lead to destruction. The desire for one cookie will lead to the desire for ten. As we indulge our desires, we replace our longing for God with satisfaction with the world, which can never truly satisfy us. No compromise.

In her book, *Love Sick: One Woman's Journey through Sexual Addiction*, Sue William Silverman writes of her addict's logic, which shares a stunning similarity to Ashley's. "It is not me—although my body is part of me—the thinner, the better. Less body, less trouble. No body. No trouble. If no man is able to see my body then I won't have to keep having sex." Ashley's addiction, if we can call it that, was perhaps the inverse of Silverman's, pivoting on the same logic. No body. No trouble. The possibility of disappearing completely or transcending all desire was far more attractive than any food.

Perhaps most striking about Ashley's story is how well she learned and followed the rules and beliefs of her religious culture. Unlike other teenagers, she was not rebellious. She was intent on following the rules as meticulously, minutely, as she could. She was convinced that the way of life offered to her by Harris and others would lead her to intimacy with God, and she was prepared to follow it to its ultimate success, the eradication of all desire, except the desire for God. Life lived this way would lead to a place of spiritual thriving.

Purity, when the word is used in the context of American youth culture, refers almost entirely to sexual abstinence—not just abstinence from a particular sexual *act*, but also a state of mind and state of being absent of sexuality. "They started talking about purity," remembers Ashley, "before I even really knew what sex was. Then we were told not to have it over and over and over. There were far more relevant things to our moral development we could have been talking about, but we weren't."

The extension of the logic of purity to food was perhaps natural. The message was to control every aspect of bodily desires, and Ashley included sexual and culinary appetites, intertwining them. Many Christian girls are on diets, of course. But they don't always give their food restrictions a religious meaning. Yet in Christian literature on sexuality, the language of food is often used to talk about sexual appetite. In one of the books in a popular series by Stephen Arterburn and Shannon Ethridge, *Every Young Woman's Battle* (the series also includes *Every Young Man's Battle* and numerous other books), there is a chapter called "The Healthy Starvation Diet." The authors do not recommend that girls starve themselves, except of all things sexual. They are advised to avoid romance novels, television soap operas, and steamy movies. They are urged to avoid all sexual thoughts. Purity demands denial of the senses and of desire.

In other words, in the culture of which Ashley was a part, girls were not only told not to have sex, but not to be sexual. As she eradicated sensual thoughts, she was driven farther away from intimacy with those around her and deeper into her own head. Intimacy would lead to the spoiling of perfection, and it was perfection for which she aimed. A person "perfect," as *Every Young Woman's Battle* put it, in "spiritual, emotional, relational, mental, and physical health," is a person free from desire.

The fantasy of the perfect self was one that Ashley clung to and lived out more than most. While this version of the self claimed to be an alternative to consumer culture, a "battle" against media images that portray girls as sexually available, it is in fact related. It relies on the same notion of perfection, a condition that can never be achieved, but must be relentlessly sought.

Ashley believed herself to be living out a protest against her culture. She was determined not to be exploited or displayed. Her body would not become a "vehicle for pleasure," not for others and not for herself. Instead Ashley worked to become a master of the will. Food was a constant, ordinary place to practice. She judged that she was doing well by the fact that her thighs did not touch each other— this was a direct indication of the control of desire. Excess of any kind, except excessive denial, was a sign that she had not given herself completely to God. The skin that filled in her upper arm and touched her rib cage was excessive flesh. Kept open, that space represented the control of desire and the growing connection between her will and God's.

In the fall of 2000, Ashley went to college. There she found herself able to hone her body even more perfectly into what she imagined was an instrument of God's will. She took up rock climbing and worked out several hours a day in the gym. Wiry and strong, she found that she had a natural talent for rock climbing, which also served as a powerful metaphor for her striving toward God.

She herself had become a hard surface, impenetrable and unmoved by desire. "I hated every ounce of nonmuscle on my body," she recalls. "I hated that I was too small to convey my strength to other people. I tried to do it through rock climbing." She wrote incessantly in her journal about her desire to give everything to God, to get rid of the self.

Privately, her friends began to worry. She was too thin, they said to each other. You could see every bone in her back. One of them decided to call Ashley's mother and talk to her about their concern. "Ashley's always been thin," her mother said. "She does get stressed out sometimes, but I don't really see anything to worry about."

The rock surface that Ashley had tried so hard to create began to crumble at a Thursday night Bible study at her college. This was a large group assembled by a charismatic local pastor for prayer, praise, and study. The "Bible study" always opened with a band playing contemporary Christian music. The students swayed to the music, as if lost in private ecstasy, until Pastor Jerry led them in collective prayer and a sermon on a biblical text. The prayer meeting had grown to more than three hundred students and had to be held in the largest auditorium on campus.

Ashley attended the prayer meeting regularly, and she involved herself deeply in the music. It was a place where communion with God could have both a private and public expression. One evening she reached her hand over her head as if to meet the music coming toward her, and then she collapsed.

The people around her did not know what to do. Some thought that she had been "slain in the Spirit" and then muttered, "Praise God!" But one of her friends said, "Call an ambulance." Ashley was carried to the hospital. No one knew what was wrong with her. The doctor blamed "stress," and Ashley was back at school the next day.

A series of collapses and then a period when she did not defecate for a week eventually led Ashley to a diagnosis. At the Mayo Clinic, she received the news: she had anorexia nervosa and pelvic floor disorder.

The news stunned Ashley. It contradicted everything she knew about the right way to live. What the doctors called "anorexia" was to her righteousness. What the doctors called "pelvic floor disorder"—a condition in which

the body is no longer capable of opening its lower aper-
tures—was the outcome of honing her will. How could it
be wrong? She had lived so meticulously by the rules that
she had been taught. She did not welcome the idea that she
had to renegotiate those rules.

At first, she simply didn't believe the doctors. She was
skeptical of all the medical personnel attending to her.
She loathed the handouts on nutrition that she was given.
Though she could see no reason why the doctors would lie
to her, she also concluded that they were wrong. How could
an anorexic be a skilled rock climber? She was strong and
healthy; they were telling her that she was sick and weak.
It made no sense.

Anorexia nervosa is often thought of as a disease created in young women by their desire to be thin and attractive. It's imagined as a response to a culture that demands
that women take up as little space as possible, that small-
ness attracts male desire. In order to be thin, young women
must not eat. Once on this path, thinness becomes its own
pursuit.

But Ashley did not want to be desired. Quite the opposite. She would have far preferred disappearing than to be
thought attractive. She did not want to be made out of flesh.
She would have preferred another, lighter substance. She
wanted to be "perfect" as her heavenly father was perfect.
And God was not of the flesh.

The first few weeks after her diagnosis were extremely
confusing. Rejecting the worldly advice of the doctors, but
newly wary of her old practices, Ashley groped for a different understanding. She had always, always wanted to
be good. Now, if she ate, she would make God unhappy,
opening the path toward unquenchable and irresistible
desires. If she did not eat, she would make her parents un-

happy, her parents who desperately wanted her to be whole and healthy, who didn't want to have to worry about her. She had only two choices: being bad or being bad. She could not see her way through the darkness that gathered around her.

In a religion class, a small light dawned. The class was reading *The Nature and Destiny of Man* by Reinhold Niebuhr, a mid-twentieth-century theologian. She encountered a phrase of Niebuhr's with a startled recognition. Niebuhr wrote that pride was only one kind of sin. The other kind of sin was self-abnegation. Ashley had been living to eliminate the self and thus to eliminate pride. But Niebuhr's suggestion that one could sin by trying too hard to avoid one's potential clicked.

It was winter and as she walked the icy paths between one building on campus and another, she kept trying this idea on. Again and again. So much of the past three years was a blank. She remembered very little; her brain had not had enough calories to store memories. She did not have enough self to hold on to a record of her own being. She read her diaries but did not find them very helpful. They were records only of her attempt to purge herself of desire, not a record of who she really was. In fact, it became obvious that Ashley had no idea who she was. Her younger self had sought only to please other people—to take care of others, not to cause trouble, to be good. Then she had become obsessed with getting rid of herself, assuming that she—whoever she was—was bad. She had no evidence that she was bad. The word *self* had had a sheen of sin on it.

As she confronted the now incontrovertible fact that she was sick and that if she didn't change, she might die, Ashley had no idea how to recover. The nutritionist at the hospital who was assigned to Ashley's case met with her weekly, and Ashley had come to dislike these meetings. The nutritionist proposed a different set of rules than the ones by which Ashley had been living, but the very idea of rules was becoming troubling to Ashley. She did not know what set of rules, what voice of regulation, to trust. The nutritionist was a heavy, middle-aged woman with an attitude that Ashley took to be condescending. As part of her recovery Ashley was supposed to write down everything that she ate or drank and bring these notes in for evaluation. One day, the nutritionist said, "You had broccoli for both lunch and dinner. Why are you eating so much broccoli?"

"I like broccoli," Ashley responded.

"You can't possibly like broccoli that much," the woman said. "That must be your anorexic voice talking."

Ashley was still very unsure of what voices in her head she should or should not listen to, but something in her said that indeed, she did like broccoli—a lot more than the salads that her anorexic self insisted on. Broccoli. She liked broccoli. Discovering this constituted a major breakthrough. She found herself rebelling against all of the new rules proposed by the nutritionist, another version of the perfect self that she was supposed to live up to. The nutritionist became just another person to please. Even though the idea was just a tiny seed inside her, she thought she needed to find another way.

She remembers a day when she sat at the kitchen table in the house she shared with several other women at the college. She had some idea that "wanting" to eat was important, but she didn't know how to put it into practice. "I think," she said to herself, "that I am hungry." Hungry—she first had to be quiet so she could experience it. Ashley did not know the sensation of hunger very well. Hunger was a desire that had to be repressed. If you paid attention to hunger, you just might satisfy it. Better to transcend the sensation and sever ties between the brain and the stomach. So as Ashley sat at the kitchen table that day, she tried to feel the sensation of hunger. She waited. There it was, a physical longing. Perhaps then, she should eat. What did she want to eat? She sat quietly. Maybe orange juice. That sounded good. She got up from the table and poured herself a glass of orange juice. She sat down again and drank it, feeling the sensation of the orange juice—the sweetness on her tongue, the coldness in her chest and then in her belly. Did something else sound good? Maybe some crackers. She ate some and noticed that she felt a little different.

Gradually, desire by desire, Ashley built herself back up. "My body was trying to talk to me, but I had to practice to hear it." She could feel hunger, and she could satisfy it. It wasn't, as she feared, that once she conceded hunger, that desire would completely overwhelm her and she would eat everything in sight. Quite the opposite. Hunger had limits, and once she paid attention, they were easy to find. As she practiced, she learned that all desires had limits and even orders. They were all essentially "good," but not every one had to be satisfied at exactly the same moment. She could put them in proper contexts—choose to satisfy one desire now or put off another for a better moment. To name and to satisfy one's desires was not, contrary to what she had long believed, to be at the mercy of selfishness and sin. On the contrary, naming and satisfying took her step-by-step onto a path toward life and goodness.

For almost a decade, Ashley had chastened her desires with the words, "Man does not live by bread alone, but by every word that proceeds from the mouth of the Lord." She had found in the self-denial of Jesus in the wilderness a model for everyday life. Now, she needed a different story. She focused on the feeding of the five thousand. In this story, Jesus takes five loaves and two fishes, borrowed from a child, and turns them into food for thousands. The story said that after everyone had had their fill, there were still baskets of food left over. Ashley found two crucial ideas in this story: one was that everyone had their fill. That meant that God respected their hunger and satisfied it. God did not ask the five thousand to go hungry in order to feed their souls. Jesus fed them, and they were satisfied. The second crucial idea was that there was still food left over. Having their fill did not mean depriving others of food. At the heart of the story was an essential abundance. If I eat, there will still be more. All will be fed.

Through these lessons on desire, food, and abundance, Ashley learned that her body was in constant communication with the good and the holy. Her body was whispering secrets of life and health, strength, and hope. If she could enter the conversation, if she could practice listening in, she, too, could draw closer to life's essential goodness. "I realized that my body was a part of me, connected to my mind and soul." The mind and soul were no longer battling to keep the body in check; instead a fluid conversation among the various parts that constituted Ashley was growing.

Sex took much longer. Anorexia had stolen Ashley's libido, and as is true of most anorexics, sexual desire was one of the last desires to return. In the end, however, sexual hunger did not turn out to be a hunger that much different from food. Like food, sexual hunger could be put into context carefully, listened to compassionately, and then responded to with joy. At first it was nearly impossible to put this into practice. Her first attempt at a boyfriend was a boy whose struggle was a lot like hers. He, too, came from a very conservative background, and he, too, could not quite grasp the idea that his body was good. Unlike

Ashley, however, he had not had to face a life-threatening illness. He had not had to walk himself through deep self-understanding to reach life. He ping-ponged between the absolute suppression of his sexual desires and the wild freedom of release. Their relationship did not last long.

She again put dating on hold, pouring herself into creative work and the friendships that she had at last started to recognize as good. Then after graduating from college, she started dating someone who did not have her same religious background. He was curious about what he considered her sexual repression, but he was respectful of it. Once he asked her why she dressed and undressed in the bathroom when they were intimate together. That was the moment she identified a voice that had long lived in her head. It was a voice that had developed over many years, culled from all the various religious influences from her youth group and her church. She called it the "Youth Leader," after all of those conversations about sex she had had in youth group. She noticed that the voice was always intent on shaming her. She learned to put Youth Leader in his place, while still listening carefully to her own life.

Several years after her recovery began, Ashley moved to a new city to begin law school. One Sunday morning as she wandered around her neighborhood, she saw a sign for a Lutheran church. Ashley had not been to a church in years, and she had grown suspicious of them. She did not want to start back down any road that might lead her to equate her body with evil, as nearly every church she had ever known had. Perhaps spiritual hunger was the last of the hungers to return, and it was a long time before she could recognize longing for God as a hunger of the body as well as of the spirit. But on the sign was a rainbow, signaling an inclusive congregation. Curious, Ashley decided to go into the church, answering a call she wasn't sure she understood.

The church was housed in an old building with a long, narrow sanctuary. She took a seat near the back, remembering that in her childhood, newcomers who didn't want attention could sit at the back and avoid conversation. But when the group began to arrive for church, there were only about twenty people, and they all sat toward the front. Hiding in the back was not an option. She sensed something that was different from both the German Lutheran insularity of her childhood and the enthusiastic pietism of her college years. If she could find words for it, she might call it a quiet joy, a community.

She learned that the church had been a Lutheran church for a century, an immigrant congregation. Then it had dwindled to just a few participants and been closed by the Lutheran leadership. But the handful of remaining parishioners had not wanted to leave their church, so they stepped outside the traditional hierarchy and called a pastor who was then on an outsiders' pastoral roster, a roster of pastors exiled for being gay. This appealed to Ashley because he seemed like he might be someone who understood the denial of the body, who might know the terrible exile from which she had come. His manner set her at ease. The liturgy gave her a place to rest. After that, she found herself wandering over to the church on Sunday mornings, learning people's names, and gradually, telling her own story. There was something about this new place that was home in a different sense. She could rediscover the essence of faith, waiting for her to find it all along. In church, the liturgy took her body through the rituals, the communion bread was broken and shared, she raised the cup to her lips. Her senses were kindled; her body was fed. Her spirit was made flesh.

Part Three

Resurrection

Monica, Paul, and Ashley all took steps toward a deeper understanding of their incarnation and so moved toward a fully embodied faith. For all of them, this path was painful and forced them to reckon with the past and the present in new ways. But Christianity doesn't end its teaching with incarnation, as important as it may be. It is also preoccupied with the equally strange and scandalous work of resurrection. Resurrection has not been an easy concept for me. I recite the Nicene Creed weekly in church that includes the words, "On the third day, he rose again in accordance with the scriptures." But I don't say them because I understand them or even believe them. I say them because I am trying to grasp them, and I sense that this grasping includes more than and perhaps supersedes my intellectual assent.

I perhaps made my greatest move toward an understanding of resurrection when, during the process of researching this book, I spent a few days at Magdalene, a sanctuary house for women in recovery for prostitution and drug addiction. At the root of every woman's story was sexual abuse—a violent taking of an elemental part of the self that had left destruction in its wake. For most women, the descent into hell was steep and long, and the hard work of resurrection is now a daily task.

One afternoon, a woman named Sheila, herself a recovering addict, took me on a tour of prostitution in Nashville. We drove through a few neighborhoods where people sat on porches or hung out on street corners. "It takes a long time sometimes," Sheila said, "for the dream of prostitution to die. Girls can start out making $100 an hour. Everyone tells them they are beautiful, and they believe it. They don't see how quickly you go from that to having your teeth fall out and begging on the street corner that you'll do anything for a dollar." Sheila sometimes goes back to her old neighborhoods with a stack of cards that have her name and telephone number on them. "When you are tired," she tells the women she meets, "call me."

Sheila then drove me out farther from the center of the city onto wide stretches of highway, past little motels and weedy lots. I realized that the hell where prostitution lives—what looked like ordinary strip malls and nameless motels to me—isn't so much a place as it is a no-place, an emptiness. That emptiness, both inside a person and outside in this dislocated landscape, breaks the body and the spirit at the same time.

I was struck by how easy it was to look around a room at a group of women and discern which ones had lived through this hell and which hadn't, which ones were finished once and for all and which ones were likely heading back, which ones had risen from the dead and were daily living their resurrection. The evidence of resurrection was written on some faces—vivid and beautiful. In those faces, I saw tenacity, grace, ferocity, and love.

What I saw at Magdalene reminded me of the stories told about Jesus's resurrection in ways that I did not expect. For example, when women come in off the streets, the first thing they usually need is nourishment. They have to be fed, and food plays a critical role in any healing. So, too, is food central to the stories of Jesus's resurrection. In one story told in the Gospel of Luke, Jesus eats a piece of broiled fish—a smoky, messy, greasy, sticky food that Jesus would have eaten with his hands, his wounded hands. In almost every story of the resurrected Jesus, food is present, and Jesus is either eating or feeding someone. Likewise, the women of Magdalene spend a good amount of time eating or feeding. They even fed me as I stood hungrily in their kitchen looking over pots of soup and pans of homemade spaghetti.

Touch also plays a critical role as the women learn, many for the first time, to be in physical contact with other people in ways that do not cause harm. Jesus, too, invited and offered touch in his "resurrection body." He gave and received hospitality—sometimes at the same moment—as in the meal shared on the road to Emmaus. He reenters the reciprocal relationships that make us human. After the cold emptiness of hell, did the warmth of broiled fish and freshly baked bread, of human friendship and contact, feel to him like it does to the women of Magdalene, like divine communication itself?

As with the women of Magdalene, Jesus still had his wounds, even after the resurrection. The physical marks of what he had suffered did not disappear, but told, physically, an important story. They were still vivid enough that he could offer to Thomas that he place his hands in the wound itself. After resurrection, the evidence of struggle and death does not disappear even as new life bursts forth.

Resurrection stories are about allowing ourselves, in spite of pain and suffering, to be vulnerable again to the world. They are about practicing hope, trust, and openness in hospitality as we go through the ordinary acts of life. And, finally, they are about working for the resurrection and liberation of others. Anyone who has made it back from the dead has something profound to teach.

The stories in this section visit darker places both in ourselves and in the American landscape. We wander farther into the margins of what I've called "exile." Each of the people in this section is primally wounded at the place of sexuality, and each one has encountered what it might mean to be made new. From their stories, we might be able to see evidence of resurrection in our own lives. Each one teaches us that being well—living whole—is demanding, harder than we imagine. Practicing resurrection means choosing to live when death would be easier, to put aside all practices of nonliving, and to let in the world and all its pain, in order, once again, to see its beauty.

Matthew

$\mathbf{W}$here should I start?" Matthew answers his own question swiftly as we sit across from each other at a small restaurant. He sighs, suggesting that he is covering overly familiar territory. "I guess I should start with my mother." In the early 1960s, when she was in her late teens, Matthew's mother became pregnant. Shamed by her family and unwilling to marry the father, she fled to California to start a new life. Matthew was born there while his mother struggled to find work and child care and make a life. "I give her a lot of credit. She struggled a lot."

Matthew's mother struggled not only financially, but also emotionally. "I guess today we would call her bipolar because her moods were all over the place. I never knew how she was going to come home. She worked hard, and I see now that she did everything she possibly could in her circumstances to give me a good life. But there were a lot of things beyond her control."

She got an education and started working long hours as a nurse, leaving Matthew in the care of neighbors. There, at age seven, Matthew was sexually molested. That began a spiraling of events that set the tone for a chaotic inner life. His mother remarried when Matthew was ten, but his new stepfather was an alcoholic, a quiet drunk who was emotionally distant. They had a child together who died when Matthew was in his early teens. Intimacy, stability, and tranquility were not states that Matthew experienced as a child.

What Matthew has come to call his sexual addiction started one day in adolescence. "My stepfather had a stash of pornographic magazines, and I found them, of course. My mother caught me with them, and she immediately took me upstairs and called some televangelist's number on the phone. She made me listen to a recorded message that said that masturbation would send me straight to hell." His stepfather took no responsibility for the magazines, denying they were his and leaving Matthew hurt and confused.

Late in Matthew's childhood, his mother had turned to televised forms of religion. In California in the 1970s, tele-religion was taking on new forms and expanding dramatically. Jim and Tammy Faye Bakker had just moved to southern California after parting bitterly with Pat Robertson's east coast Christian Broadcasting Network. Together with their friends Jan and Paul Crouch, they were preparing to launch a new network, Trinity Broadcast Network, that would become Matthew's mother's favorite. Jim and Tammy Faye left TBN quickly after another conflict with the Crouches, but TBN thrived nonetheless through tireless fund-raising. Matthew's mother loved the worship and praise music, the energetic preaching, and the preachers' silky voices. She loved the soft crinoline dresses the women wore and their sparkly eye shadow. All life's edges appeared soft on TBN. She saw on television something she longed to have: an ordered world where opulence, beauty, and righteousness went together. She began to turn to the television for various kinds of help, including the hotline numbers by the telephone.

The kind of religion that played on Matthew's family television all day and into the night was a series of contradictions that offered Matthew an odd picture of holiness. On the one hand, television preachers and their cadres made every effort to be personal. Preachers and their wives spoke directly to the camera offering help to their viewers, pleading with them to send a little money to help the ministry, to stay in personal contact. They claimed to know their viewers' hearts and know God's very own plan.

At the same time, a great deal of what went on was obviously fake, a shimmery fakeness that was all but intentional. The dealings were shady and secret, always marred by whisperings of scandal. Television ministries were and continue to be plagued by sexual and financial scandal in particular. In the early 1980s, Jim Bakker was accused of having had a sexual liaison with a church secretary named Jessica Hahn. Hahn said that she had been drugged and raped by Bakker and his friend John Fletcher. Paul Crouch, many years later, was accused of firing a male employee after having a sexual relationship with him. Bakker spent time in prison for fraud while the Crouches have never been formally investigated. TBN remains extremely low on any scale for financial transparency.

While hypocrisy might be easy to see in televangelists like the Bakkers and the Crouches, we might also think about the religious atmosphere they helped create. Albeit saccharine, they added an element of sensuality to traditional straight-laced, hell and damnation Protestant revivalism. For Matthew's mother, the music was especially important in giving her a sense that God wanted to shower her with blessings, that God promised freedom from her personal chaos. Set up against other fiery and manly preachers of the day like Jerry Falwell and Oral Roberts, Jim Bakker was effeminate. He did not embody the "muscular Christianity" that was important to his contemporaries. Both Bakker and Crouch, it was frequently hinted, were homosexuals.

Perhaps to remedy this perceived fault, in a business where image is everything, John Fletcher arranged the incident with Hahn. While Hahn and Bakker agree about little else that happened that night, they both agree that Bakker was involved in order to "feel like a man." The trap that Bakker found himself in is one that is perhaps not at all uncommon in American Protestant Christianity and explains, in part, why scandal plays such a central role. To prove one's masculinity, one has to break the very rules that the faith insists sets it apart. Masculinity and religiosity are pitted against each other. And all men in Matthew's environment had secrets.

For Matthew, that secret was pornography. As he grew older, damnation or no damnation, that fascination intensified. No matter how he tried, he could not get himself on the "straight path." Ironically, while he chastised himself for always going astray, he was perhaps as good a student of his culture as could be. In this religious environment, all intimacy was airbrushed and image-oriented. It was performed more than experienced. What was said and what was done were not the same. The image projected on the screen and the one behind the scenes didn't match. It was eerily similar to the life that Matthew was building for himself: an outside Matthew and an inside Matthew. Televised religion, like pornography, made promises it couldn't fulfill and told stories of a fantasy life that remained largely empty.

"Going astray" was central to the religious and sexual dynamic. The greater the man, the more powerful his secret. The more dangerous and potent its revelation. Between the example of televangelists and the example of his stepfather, Matthew received the idea that sex was a secret you kept from the people closest to you. In some ways, secret pleasures were allowed, even necessary, so long as they remained secret. In the end, pornography continued to have a draw for Matthew that he couldn't explain, about which he felt terribly guilty, but whose roots were deeper than he could tease out.

Matthew's mother eventually accepted an invitation to a Bible study, and she and Matthew became involved in the Vineyard Movement, a distinctive group of charismatic Christians whose version of Christianity was making a meteoric rise in the 1970s. Even though the Vineyard Movement was like other Pentecostal and revival movements that had come before it, it was also very much of its own time and place: southern California circa 1978, coinciding directly with Matthew's teenage years. The Bible studies and worship services were full of contemporary lingo, shaggy-haired young people, popular styles of music, waving of hands, and attempts to feel the Holy Spirit working. Matthew went down on his knees early and gave his life to God.

At the Vineyard, church was designed around intimate and experiential Christianity that resonated with both Matthew and his mother. They believed in healing, in transformation, and in the mighty power of the Holy Spirit. The Vineyard emphasized a direct and personal relationship between the believer and the Holy Spirit. On the one hand, it advocated the tremulous emotionalism of Pentecostalism. Vineyard leaders wanted people to get carried away with the power of God. On the other hand, leaders publicly struggled with such displays when people seemed obligated to perform them.

One of the key figures in the music developing out of

the Vineyard movement was Larry Norman whose song "Why Should the Devil Have All the Good Music?" embodied a new era of Christian music. Norman, Vineyard founder John Wimber, and others wanted to bring the vitality of contemporary music to Christianity. Vineyard-style worship services used electric guitars, keyboards, and drums. They put simplified Bible passages to singable, danceable, swayable tunes.

People flocked to the Vineyard, but this particular aspect of its work brought a hailstorm of critics. Jerry Falwell denounced the new music as "a sinful compromise with worldliness and immoral sensuality." Merely changing the lyrics didn't make such music holy. Many argued that such music put Christianity in danger of capitulating to the world. The "world" meant, as Falwell's words suggest, at least in part sex. In conservative Christianity at the time, it wasn't unusual to hear people argue that the rhythms of rock-and-roll music aroused sensuality and caused promiscuity. They objected to having this music in sacred settings. At the same time, Wimber, Norman, and others were having a profound influence that spread rapidly through conservative, Pentecostal, and even fundamentalist circles.

Matthew fervently hoped that in giving his life to God he could put the past behind him. He believed that the promised transformation was real and would take effect. He prayed. He clung hard to this new truth. But even in the midst of this religious transformation, Matthew couldn't stem the tide. His parents were nearly completely withdrawn from the grief of losing their child. Matthew still found himself at parties where he knew he didn't belong. One night, at one such party, when Matthew was high, an older man took him into a bedroom and raped him. The unstable, fragile world that Matthew inhabited rent itself finally in two. He didn't speak of the rape to anyone. He blamed himself, called the rape the "wages of sin" to himself, and vowed again to turn his life around. When the raw pain subsided, what was left was an aching emptiness that nothing seemed to fill. He'd learned in church that Jesus was supposed to fill that vacuum, heal his broken heart, and change his life. But the emptiness did not give way.

Sometimes it would yawn so wide that Matthew felt he needed something, anything, that worked faster than religion. One outlet was drugs, but another, one that worked better and without a hangover, was pornography. Each episode with pornography began with a dull hunger, a kind of persistent ache that repeatedly demanded satisfaction. Even as he said no to it, the itch grew stronger and began to shut out all other thoughts. Eventually, he would give in to it. He had a stash of pornographic magazines, and once he could drive, he also drove to porn shops far from his house in neighborhoods where no one knew him. Brief satisfaction of the hunger was followed by a wave of contrition and deep shame. "That's the last time," he said to himself a thousand times. Repentance and recommitment brought a period of calm, until once again, his hunger grew.

By the time Matthew was seventeen, his world had two distinct realms: the public worship of Jesus and the deep privacy of pornography. The bridge between these two was shame. This pattern, one he would not recognize for many years, shaped his entire life. Church promised freedom from shame, but still somehow fed it. Pornography promised another kind of freedom, but never delivered. Pornography drove him to church, and church back to pornography.

Matthew was seventeen when he met Katie, a girl at

the Vineyard with whom he felt an electric connection. The two of them started lingering together after worship services. Sometimes Matthew drove her home. Katie came from circumstances very different from Matthew's. Her parents had come to the Vineyard through fundamentalism. They were firm believers in the Rapture and in prophecy, and they were seeking a sense of revival through the Vineyard.

Katie had given her heart to Jesus at age eight. She'd been baptized at age twelve. Matthew was her first boyfriend. Matthew had a hint of the bad boy about him. She knew his family life had been rough. But most of what she saw in him, she admired. He had a "passion for the Lord." He had a strong walk with God, she thought. She saw his conversion to Christianity as a triumph over the pain of his past, as evidence of the power of the Holy Spirit.

Matthew and Katie's early sexual life acted out a very complex script, each of them with only partial recognition of their roles. Katie knew that she was supposed to be desirable and to resist Matthew's desire. Matthew also had to express and repress desire simultaneously. So ingrained was the pattern that Matthew had already associated with sex—sin, repentance, hope, calm, hunger, sin, and so on—that it shaped their sexual interactions as well. Matthew would make an advance. Katie would resist it. They both would feel guilty. They would confess their sins to God, pray together, recommit themselves to putting Jesus at the center of their relationship, and willfully cool things off until the next episode.

The result was that over the three years that they dated before they got married, Matthew and Katie did a lot of heavy petting for which they thought they should repent, but weren't sure. They could say, at least "in a technical sense," as Matthew put it, that they were still virgins. Meanwhile, Katie knew nothing of the sexual abuse, the rape, the pornography, nothing of Matthew's dark side that he was trying so desperately to purge.

Matthew and Katie lived in a religious environment that was trying to borrow heavily from cultural trends in order to draw people toward Christianity, while at the same time resisting the sexual and worldly charge that shaped the very trends they were adopting. It made for a strange atmosphere. On the one hand, the world was roundly rejected and condemned. On the other, it was embraced for "relevance" and a contemporary freshness. In the decades before Matthew and Katie's wedding, the prevailing Christian attitude toward sex was that it was something men wanted and women conceded. Men needed to tame their sexual desires in order to fit God's plan; women needed to be careful not to lead men into sin. Rigid roles for men and women, and fear of the consequences of sinful sex shaped the landscape.

But these views were under revision. While they were by no means discarded, the conversation about the relationship between sex and God was changing. The book that perhaps marks this change most directly is Tim and Beverly LaHaye's *The Act of Marriage*, published in 1972 after much resistance from the Christian publishing industry. This book was shocking for its explicit discussion of the details of sexual acts. It was shocking, too, for its emphasis on female pleasure.

The book begins with a sexy warning that this book is only to be handled by married people or those about to be married. It advises that engaged couples read the book separately. The LaHayes taught that sex, by which they meant heterosexual intercourse, was good and natural and that its use in marriage was for the pleasure of both men and women. The book went further, in fact, arguing that sex was the "most thrilling, exciting, and fulfilling experience in the world (if done properly)." In other words, sexual intercourse had gone from being a necessary evil to a state of idyllic fantasy. Married people were now obligated to do it "properly" in order to fully experience God's love for them. Not only could marital sex be perfected, that was in fact God's plan. Anything short of God-ordained ecstasy was a personal failing.

For Matthew and Katie, this idealized version of marital sex spelled disaster. They each came into marriage with private burdens. Sexuality was a language they fumbled in speaking to each other. The sinister part of the idealization of Christian marriage was that it wasn't regarded as an idealization. It was regarded as an expectation. If you could only follow the rules and do it right, you could have this pure, ecstatic experience, as the LaHayes led you to believe they had. In that, *The Act of Marriage* shared a startling similarity with pornography: it was titillating and based on fantasy.

What then, for Matthew and Katie, when they discovered that sex is not the "most thrilling, exciting, and fulfilling experience"? Who did they have to blame? Themselves? Or each other? For Matthew and Katie, this teaching had early consequences. Neither of them was prepared for the demands of intimacy that marriage required. Katie was intimidated. She did not know how to move from the well-practiced avoidance of sexual feelings to freedom. She knew how to police herself, but she had not anticipated how difficult it would be to let go. There were other conflicts as well. Christian culture taught her that she should, in the LaHayes' words, "clean up, fix up, paint up" in order to remain attractive to her husband. In other words, she was supposed to remain in a semi-idealized state for him at all times, while at the same time, she was somehow supposed to let go completely into marital bliss. From Matthew, she also received a message that confused her: no matter how hard she tried, she was never open enough to him. He seemed always dissatisfied with their level of intimacy. She lived with a latent sense of unmet expectations, of inadequacy and uncertainty. Of failure.

Matthew, meanwhile, had been certain that marriage "as God intended" would finally put to rest the chaos inside him. He would no longer desire pornography. He would find ecstasy, bliss, and intimacy in perfect union with his perfect bride. He would no longer drive across town to fulfill his secret desires. There would be no more "stash." His wedding would mark the end of that period of his life. It was just a phase after all, a substitute for the real thing. Marriage, as he saw it, was a kind of salvation. "And it worked," Matthew said with a wry smile. "For about two weeks."

Matthew continued, "We were taught that a person should stay sexually pure until marriage, as my wife did. Or tried to if it hadn't been for me. I think about how deeply we believed that and how much we struggled with it when we were young. But now I wonder, for what? Why should Katie have had to go through that? So that she could get messed up by a guy with a raging, unacknowledged sex addiction? Is that what sexual purity is for? What about a process of self-discovery and self-understanding before marriage? Why don't they teach that?"

Matthew and Katie found their marriage in trouble early, although it took them both a long time to acknowledge that. Katie could not free herself emotionally or physically. She found the pleasure that she had long denied was now stingy. She couldn't convince herself to feel very much. Matthew had had shame and self-disgust as constant companions for so long that he did not find them willing to depart. He loved Katie and wanted to be the partner she deserved, but every lapse into old habits was cause for shame. Shame caused a desire to escape or an opportunity to blame Katie for what ailed him.

Marriage, for all its promises, changed little in Matthew's interior world. As before, church and pornography held it up. Each one promised but did not deliver. Church promised the bedrock of God's truth. Pornography promised a connection to a remote part of himself that with each episode seemed to bob to the surface and then disappear into the deep. As he constantly policed the boundary that would allow him to continue to live in this dark place, fear of discovery was always with him.

While many people talk about pornography as a problem of desire—misplaced or uncontrollable desire—for Matthew the bigger problem was intimacy. Pornography had provided Matthew a safe place, deep inside himself, for pleasure. But the connection to another human being was part of the fantasy. Images of naked strangers could not hurt, reject, or shame him. Nakedness provided the illusion of openness, as if the woman whose photo he looked at was making herself available to him. Pornography had the capacity to make him feel both fleetingly alive and simultaneously numb. Fantasy replaced the nuanced intimacy demanded of him in his everyday life. "I always imagined this woman who could be completely open to me. Who didn't have anything holding her back, didn't carry any baggage. Every time I opened a magazine or drove to a porn shop or went online, I was always looking for her. And she was never there." The woman Matthew imagined was something like the LaHayes' idealized wedding-night bride. Both were unencumbered and unashamed. Both had the capacity to be completely open sexually. Both held Katie to an impossible standard. Matthew's religious beliefs about marriage and his addiction to pornography fed each other constantly, like two twin monsters.

But for all the difficulty, Matthew and Katie's marriage continued. They had three children, moved into a suburban house, started and maintained careers. They each worked to send the other through various degree programs. They sent their children to a Christian school and attended a large, suburban church. They were no longer Vineyard charismatics, but more straightforward evangelicals. They knew how to raise their hands in worship, but few in their congregation ever passed out from contact with the Holy Spirit or performed miraculous acts of healing. They attended a couples' Bible study, and Katie taught Sunday school. Much of Matthew's life was utterly and completely "normal." It was the normal that he himself had not known in childhood. For Matthew, this ability to provide stability for his children was a considerable triumph. Yet he was far from being the person he wanted to be. And the advent of the Internet made his addiction all that much easier to feed.

"It got bad. I was looking at pornography when I should have been taking care of my kids. I would have sex with my wife and then go online and look at pornography. I was always two people instead of one. I didn't want to admit that I, the good Christian husband and father, was also the dirty man, the porno addict, the guy slinking around in a trench coat."

❦

Matthew and Katie eventually sought marriage counseling, knowing that something was wrong in their marriage and always had been. In an individual session with the counselor, Matthew confessed his attachment to pornography. The counselor was the first person he had ever told. The therapist recommended a twelve-step sex addiction group, an idea that Matthew resisted. Matthew didn't see himself like other addicts. For one thing, he was a committed Christian, and Christ, not the twelve steps, was supposed to set him free. The fact that God had failed to do so just meant that perhaps Matthew was too despicable a sinner to be bothered with or that God was still too angry with him. How the twelve steps could accomplish something that the Lord of the Universe couldn't or wouldn't seemed like nonsense to Matthew.

But eventually, sensing his life was out of control and wanting desperately to change, Matthew parked his car one night outside St. Anthony's Episcopal Church and for a few minutes watched while people approached the door. Under the street lamp, he tried to study their faces. After a while, he pulled his key out of the ignition and went in. This was unquestionably the start of something new.

When Matthew was young, few people would have talked about or acknowledged something called sexual addiction. Until recently, addiction was understood primarily as a chemical reaction to a chemical substance. Alcohol and drugs fit this model perfectly. Sexual feelings and actions are a less sure fit. But the part-spiritual, part-medical understanding of addiction formed by twelve-step groups offered the ability to name the loss of a sense of control, the inability to will an end to something that threatened to destroy one's life.

Though Matthew was distrustful of the secular content of the twelve steps, in fact, a good deal in Alcoholics Anonymous was familiar to his evangelical worldview. The twelve steps had been initially explicitly Christian. The model is similar in some ways to the one that Matthew had encountered long ago. It involves a confession of sin and acceptance of the fact that salvation is not yours to achieve, but is given to you by the grace of God. But the founders of Alcoholics Anonymous wanted to transform this very specific Christian language into a broad, almost secular vocabulary so that it could be of use to the greatest number of people. And, in fact, this is what they accomplished. "Sin" became "addiction"; "God" became "Higher Power, as I understand Him"; and so on.

Addressing sex as an addiction is problematic. As Matthew said, "It's one thing to stop drinking alcohol. You don't need alcohol. Alcohol isn't a biological drive. But sex is something really close to the core of who you are. Sex addiction is a lot harder to deal with because it feeds off something that is really basic."

Despite having some medical foundation, addiction doesn't require a diagnosis. In AA terms, it is a problem if it causes a problem. No doctor can give you a test to find out if you are addicted or not. And what constitutes "addiction" for one person may not for another. AA's mantra that it is a problem if it causes a problem is a pretty low bar. In Matthew's case the problems were deeply internal. On the surface, he had a marriage that had lasted for more than twenty years, children he loved deeply and who loved him, a steady job, and career plans. His "problem" was that he loathed himself.

At root this was, Matthew now believes, a spiritual problem. In his Sex Addicts Anonymous group, he could address it because there were concrete actions that he could take to keep himself sober while looking at underlying causes for his behavior. At first, however, he found himself uncomfortable. He wanted to distance himself from what he considered the "wimpy" language of "Higher Power." "See, I'd already found God, I thought. I already knew the truth. I had accepted Jesus into my heart, and I'd been a Christian for a long time. I just thought that God despised me. But at least I had religious truth, unlike these others."

Matthew was desperate enough to heal his inner life that he kept going to meetings. He saw enough transformation with the people in the group that he was hopeful for himself. Gradually, something dawned on him. His God, the one he felt so much shame in front of, the one who seemed to heap burning coals on his head, was a strange friend of his addiction. The two of them had conspired to keep him imprisoned.

"I was criticizing that guy over there for his wimpy New Age 'Higher Power,' but eventually I had to admit that whomever that guy was praying to, he was sober. And however powerful and truthful I said my God was, He wasn't getting me out of my addiction. I didn't have a faith that worked, a faith that could keep me sober."

The faith that he had to climb toward was one in which God might actually love him. He had to find a God who stood by him in struggle and did not flee. Matthew still had years of struggle ahead of him. The new life he could now envision was a very slow dawn. But gradually, a "faith that works," rooted in grace, trust, and acceptance, rooted in a God of startling love, came to take its place in Matthew and bring him back to life. This new life is not free from pain and fear. But he has learned to lean in instead of flee, to use his deep wounds as an opportunity to listen for the grace of God.

One critical shift in Matthew's life was learning to sit with and accept pain, through a practice that is like contemplative prayer. Matthew no longer tries to make the feelings of loss, despair, and aching loneliness go away. He doesn't have a remedy for them. No quick fix. Instead, he has learned to sit still with them.

"You know how you can first feel a train coming from a long way off, from way down on the tracks? The first shudder, the first movement on the ground? That's what I have learned to listen for. The train is all of the old fear and pain and loneliness, and the urge to do something about it, to run away, to escape it comes with it. What I have learned to do is to stand there and let it come. I let the train come through. I let it shake the ground around me, fill my ears with its noise while I stay still. Eventually, it moves on. The hardest thing I know is to let the train come through and not run away. But I have learned that that is the only way to live."

Genevieve

This story begins, for me, in a sunny courtyard in Nashville on a spring afternoon where a woman I'll call Genevieve was having a cigarette and talking about her new job. The courtyard had a vine-covered stone wall and a flowering cherry tree. An afternoon breeze blew through, turning the patio into a small piece of paradise. As I sat with Genevieve, I felt grateful to be accepted on an ordinary lawn chair on an ordinary afternoon, but I also felt the edgy sensation of not really belonging. I was an interloper, maybe even worse, a reporter. I wanted information, stories, the goods. On another level, I didn't only want information that I could use. I wanted to connect. I wanted to understand and even to be a part of something that had already filled me with awe. But I was decidedly uncomfortable—painfully aware of the color of my skin, of the ease and unearned privilege of my experience relative to the hell that the women I had joined here had been through. It hurt to sit there, and I cannot deny that part of me wanted to run away. I counseled myself to breathe deeply, to sit still, and to wait.

Eventually, Genevieve and I were alone in the courtyard, and she began to talk. As her story unfolded, a sense of honor, of holiness took the place of my nervousness. I wanted the afternoon to stretch on endlessly, so that I could soak it in. The story was a gift I did not feel I deserved to receive. I still handle it restlessly, wanting to do it justice, but fearful that I never can.

❦

Genevieve grew up in a small town in Tennessee, and her early life was chaotic. Her mother drank heavily; there were always people in her house, parties, fights, noise, drunkenness. She hid in the back bedroom. She had a favorite hiding spot under the bed where no one could find her, she imagined. She created there a secret world where everything was just the way she wanted it to be, a fantasy. She had pretty dresses and beautiful jewelry. People always commented how pretty she was and how much they liked her. Her reality was that hiding under the bed amidst the dust bunnies was a good place to be. As good as it got.

With her little sister, she often went to church, as almost everyone in her small town did. It was tradition, an expectation. Her mother sent the children with various relatives, and even went herself when she was sober, which Genevieve said wasn't very often. The church was a little Baptist church, not far from her home, so the children could walk there, down a dirt road and up the worn wooden steps, through the big front doors.

The preacher was a traditional Baptist with a booming voice and a fire-and-brimstone message about the doom and destruction of sinners. When he spoke, he sometimes seemed like the voice of God himself, and the people in the church revered him. She also learned to fear God in that most basic sense. God was someone who was "gonna git you" if you weren't good. Salvation was a matter of being good, of being inside the grace of God. This wasn't an easy place to stay because, she learned, we have sinful natures, but it was imperative. Without it, only hell awaited, the fiery pit. The other message she received from church, which also didn't prove to be of much use, was that your parents are responsible for your salvation until you are twelve years old, and then you are on your own. After that, you had to make a decision for Christ or end up roaming in the outer darkness.

The theology Genevieve learned was an otherworldly theology that promised rewards or punishment in the ever after for behavior here on earth. It imagined a realm of choice—as if life were a road lined with dangerous twists and turns, perilous possibilities that could carry a person to hell or to heaven, with hell the most likely option. People dressed up carefully to go to church. The women wore hats with feathers. The men wore suits and ties. Their clothes glittered, as if they were trying to attract the attention of God with their prettiness or distract God from their sins.

The problem was that the question of heaven or hell, of "leaning on the Lord's side" as the Gospel song said, was a heavy responsibility that little Genevieve took seriously, and at the same time, her world was rapidly disintegrating, just at the moment when the preacher said everything ultimately became her "choice." The church was of little use in that disintegration. She could see that on the road to heaven or hell, hell was rapidly gaining.

One of the men who frequently came to the house started "messing with her" when she was tiny. That reality was so common, so unremarkable, that no one noticed or cared. She learned that her body wasn't her own, that she had no say over who touched her and who did not. That no one would help or save her if the touching hurt. She learned that her parents or her family—her aunts, uncles, cousins—would not protect and care for her, no matter what the church said was right.

By the time she was twelve, the magical "age of decision," her mother saw her as a tool to be used—although her mother's chaos made it impossible to see anything clearly. Her mother did the unthinkable: she sold her to a man. She didn't and still doesn't know the details of their arrangement. It feels like the devil himself snuck in and struck the deal that shaped the rest of her life. The fatal "choice" was his, not hers.

One day she was at home, and the next day she was in a car with a man whom she had seen around some. She learned that he was a "pimp," even though she didn't know what a pimp was, and that she was supposed to do things with men when he told her to. If her world had before had points of light—playing with her little sister in the woods behind their house, the smile of her fifth-grade teacher that could light up a room, the Sunday school teacher who smelled like rosewater and fried chicken—those lights flickered out. The pimp sold her to a couple—a man and a woman—who took her across the state line, kept her in a hotel room, and raped her repeatedly. For decades, what happened in that hotel room was Genevieve's most terrible and secret shame. She did not know how to find words for it, and when she did find words, they were stark and violent words: "I was forced to give head, to suck on an ugly, old woman's pussy," she says. "The girl who was raped was my little girl," Genevieve now says. "She is still wild and angry."

The next three decades are a blur, a long nightmare. She lived in Tennessee, in Virginia, in North Carolina for a short time. There were moments when she could imagine her life as glamorous, when she could imagine that people wanted to buy sex from her because she was beautiful. The culture around her cultivated this idea through television, movies, and magazines: sex between strangers is supposed to be exciting. Prostitution is a very complicated reality. It is insidious, reaching a person in the deepest, darkest, quietest places of her life. Much later, when Genevieve was in recovery, she had to take long, painful looks at herself, at the prostitute inside of her that had shaped some of her earliest memories and earliest understandings of herself.

Genevieve could begin to think prostitution was normal, just the way that the world is, a fact of survival. It didn't matter, just like her body didn't matter. If she could get what she wanted or what she needed from selling her body, what difference did it make? Along the way, her teeth fell out, her body ached, and her health deteriorated. Prostitution is not what it looks like on television—sudden, anonymous encounters between beautiful people. It teaches you that your body is trash, that you are not worth anything. It leaves scars that are so immense, they reach through the whole of a person. People who want anonymous sex want it for reasons—usually their own dark and painful reasons—that make anonymity a curse.

Genevieve remembers these years as dark, dreary, and streaked with a deep hunger for drugs that kept her on the move. She had four children, all four of them the children of her pimp, all four born in the hazy unreality of which her life consisted. By the time she had her youngest son, she had dumped all of her kids on her family so many times, they wouldn't take them anymore. She would say, "I'm going to the store," and not come back for months or years. So when she had the last baby, if she said, "I'm going to the store," her family said, "You take him with you." So he went with her everywhere—to the store, to the bar, to the dope house. She would put juice and a cookie in his hand and disappear into the back room. "I hate that now," she said with particular passion.

In Nashville, prostitutes work long stretches of empty road and highway underpasses. They work from weedy lots and boxlike motels; they stand aimlessly along bus routes, staring out into nothing or sit on the steps of crumbling buildings. The world has an absence of beauty. Still, there is a dream in prostitution, an ideal that works to keep a person from ever facing the truth. That one day, you'll be able to buy your way out, that other people want and admire what you have, that there is glamour and desire in every encounter. It took a long time for that "dream" to fade.

"I had no idea," Genevieve said, "from inside that hole, what the world was actually like." She showed me with cigarette ashes how much crack two dollars would buy. If someone is begging for two dollars, she said, they are really, really sick. Desperate. They aren't really getting high. They are just getting the idea of high. She used to go to the dope man with eighty cents or sixty cents and beg for just that much crack.

Genevieve was in and out of jail when she heard about a program called Magdalene. At Magdalene, the women are given housing, food, medical care, money for shampoo, and even Diet Pepsis, and anything else they need to get well. For a long time, she didn't see herself as someone who needed a program like that. She was fine. Hidden underneath that arrogance was another voice that said she wasn't worth it, that if they knew, if they really knew, who she had been, they would turn her away, just like sometimes in her dreams, she was turned away from the door of the church. But eventually, her desperation grew. She had the tiniest seed of longing to be someone different, if not for herself, then for her kids.

In the first stage of the program, she was required to go to ninety meetings for drug addiction in ninety days. She saw doctors, dentists, and therapists. She got "clean" in more senses than one. She slept in the safe house at first and then moved on to one of the Magdalene houses where she had a room to come back to every night. At first, the struggle was simply to get well enough to think clearly. Then came intense waves of emotion, pain that seemed like it would never end. She stayed with it because she was so desperate to get well that she would have done anything. "If they told me to go stand up on that building for thirty-seven hours and then I would be clean, I would've done it."

Every morning, the women gathered in a circle to talk about how to get well. At first, even after she had been sober for a while, Genevieve sat with her arms crossed staring into the void in front of her. "I don't have to tell those bitches anything about me. They don't need to hear my story," she decided. When it was her turn to speak, she looked to the side, shifted in her chair, and spoke vaguely of her struggles.

Day after day, however, she gathered in the circle and listened. She gradually noticed that the women who told their stories were getting freer. You could see the weight lifting off of them. Secrets were burdens, some of them so heavy they were crushing the people who held on to them. People who told their stories looked lighter; they were getting better. When she finally told her story, she said, "It was like losing thirty pounds." She also saw how her story could help other people. People would say, "That happened to me, and I couldn't tell anyone anything about it." Or, "That happened to my niece or my daughter, and I had almost given up on her." She gradually saw, with a spark of hope, that it might be that her story was not for her alone. It might be of use. Yes, she had suffered, but that was not the end.

At Magdalene, they had a special group to deal with the addiction of prostitution. Reclaiming oneself is a long and grueling project. Prostitution isn't just an act: it is an emotional, spiritual, and physical reality. To be free from it, Genevieve found she had to reconstruct her understanding of the world from the ground up. What was a relationship? What was another person? How does a person learn to care enough about herself that quick money stops looking good? Genevieve had to acknowledge the fact that she still fantasized about prostitution; that for all its horror, it had been a way that she had "felt good" about herself. When the women gathered for "prostitution group" with a strong, formidable recovering prostitute named Regina, they were often visibly uncomfortable. They would leave their notebooks and homework in their rooms on purpose. One woman said to Regina, "This group really pisses me off." Regina shot back quickly, "That's because you have to face yourself."

Facing oneself is hard, daily, agonizing work. Genevieve was eighteen months clean when she got married to a man that she had known for eight years. Everything was still hard—being married, staying clean. As soon as she got married, she started finding other men attractive. She knows this is lust: "It's the enemy's way of trying to get me lined up on his side again. He is cunning and powerful. He knows my weaknesses."

In Magdalene, Genevieve encountered new ways to think about God. Maybe instead of being out to get her, God was someone who loved her, who was strong enough to see and hear it all and still come out loving. Genevieve sees herself "walking toward God." She is determined in Bible study and has a teacher in the Church of Christ. She wants to evangelize, to reach people with this powerful love of God, and she is concerned about losing her street language. She wants to keep a way of speaking that will help her help others. That involves swearing; she is conflicted about the swearing though, because she is trying to live a "Christ-like life." She knows that addicts don't listen to someone who hasn't been there and who cannot speak the harsh language of the streets. It doesn't matter how many degrees you have or what you think you know. They can easily dismiss you if you don't know what it is like.

The woman who founded Magdalene, Becca Stevens, has been a powerful beacon for Genevieve. Once, Genevieve went to Becca's church and saw her preach. Becca stood up barefoot "in front of all of those old, white people." At first, Genevieve found herself too busy judging everyone around her to pay attention, but when she finally starting paying attention, she said she saw a halo around Becca's head and felt the power of her holiness. "My hair started tingling and that's how I know the Holy Spirit is present."

Genevieve believes that truth will set her free, but she also knows that it is a gradual process, not something that happens all at once. One thing she still is not ready to do is tell her children that they are the product of her prostitution. She knows that if at least one son knew, he would kill his father. She has told them, "There isn't anything that I wouldn't do for dope." She has left it to them to fill in the blanks. She doesn't think they can hear it. She has told them that she would braid the dope men's hair and clean the dope men's house. They have an image of her as just being someone who hung around the dope men, not someone who gave them oral sex and "lay down with them" for drugs. Their father was her pimp, and he is still a pimp. They know him, and they know that he is a pimp, but they just don't put all of the information together. She says she understands that. She struggles to put all the information together as well, when there is something that she doesn't want to see.

She now believes God was with her at every turn in her life, at every dark and hopeless moment, and that it was just a question of recognizing it. She believes in God's mercy and God's forgiveness. She repeats, "God is good." When Genevieve came in from the darkness, she did not have any trust in herself, and she still doesn't. All trust is for God. "We've done things my way. Now I know that you must humble yourself. You simply must humble yourself."

Genevieve now works with other women who are trying to get well. She is on her feet all day, every day. She hardly has a moment to answer her phone when it rings, and she keeps herself focused on giving away what she has been given. Genevieve believes that our stories, as much as we pay dearly for them, end up not being ours. We have stories, but only so that we can tell them to others and use them to aid others. They do not, finally, belong to us.

Becca

Unlike many of the people who agreed to be a part of this book, Becca Stevens does not want to remain anonymous. She has told her story hundreds of times and is the author of numerous books. She finds the veil of anonymity discomfiting, as if in it she might lose herself. Becca is the chaplain at Vanderbilt University and the founder of a sanctuary program in Nashville, Tennessee, for women coming out of drug abuse and prostitution, women who are among the most damaged by our culture's toxic treatment of sexuality. For Becca, the "original sin" of our society is sexual abuse, and she shares that pain with the women of Magdalene. By "original sin," she means that sexual abuse is an overlooked but central part of who we are as a society. At least sixty million survivors of sexual abuse live in the United States today, and sexual abuse affects one in every four girls and one in every six boys. But it isn't even the rampancy of sexual abuse that Becca points to, so much as the fact that sexual abuse wounds a child at the very center of their personhood. If sexuality is the place where a person—body, mind, and spirit—is integrated and holds together, then sexual abuse takes a person apart and scatters her. The process of reintegration is lifelong.

When I asked Becca for this interview, I felt awkward. She has authored her own story many times. By no means does she need me to tell it for her. She also challenged me before we even began: "The people who are in this book are offering you the precious pearls of their stories. What are you offering them?" Her challenge was a reminder that, while seeking our own healing is good and necessary work, there is much more to be done. In concrete and tangible ways, we must be extending hospitality and healing to others. Telling stories is wonderful, but working to heal the rift in our church and our society that daily damages precious human beings is better. She consented to the interview because it fit with her overall understanding of the work that she is committed to. "I will do anything to help us get better—us being the church, the community, and the society."

Becca's parents came from the Northeast to the South in 1967 when Becca was four years old. Her father was the rector at a small mission church in Nashville, and he and his wife and five children had just settled into the rectory next to the Episcopal church when he was struck and killed by a drunk driver. The day was November 22, 1968, her mother's birthday. Her father had gone to a mid-morning Eucharist service and had decided that he should stop off to see a couple who were in the midst of a marital crisis. After a visit at their house, he was driving home to spend the day with his family when he was struck by a semitruck. The driver of the semi had two prior drunk driving convictions but still had his commercial license.

Her mother had five young children to raise and nowhere to go. Her own parents were dead. She had a brother in New York, but he wasn't able to help. The church agreed to sell her the rectory, and she continued to live there for all of Becca's growing-up years. Her mother, a woman that

Becca admires for her strength and endurance, worked at a community center for children, and Becca spent her time between church, home, school, and the diverse neighborhoods of north Nashville.

Becca's father's death wasn't the only death in the church that year. Three months later, another man in the church, who had been a friend of her father's, died suddenly, perhaps of a heart attack, when his car careened off a road. "The church was reeling," Becca remembers. The losses were mounting. Months later, when Becca was six years old, another man in the church, also a friend of her father's and the church's senior warden, called her into a side room in the upstairs part of the fellowship hall. The fellowship hall was a detached building, an old house that had been gutted and designed for church functions. The grown-ups often sent the kids upstairs with their plates of spaghetti, while they ate downstairs. Becca remembers that there were several children upstairs, including her siblings, when "Mr. Johnson" called her into one of the small rooms off of the main room. He shut the door. Her six-year-old memory did not retain what exactly he said, and she had no words for what he did until much later. She remembers that she never dropped or set down the plate that she was holding. Later, when she confronted him as an adult and as a priest, he said, "That first day I just rubbed myself between your legs," as if, somehow, to justify the action.

Becca wonders what it was about the church that allowed Mr. Johnson's abuse of her to continue unabated. Was it that people in the South in those days had an indelible respect for authority, for men who looked like they were supposed to be in charge? Was it that men like Mr. Johnson owned the church, were its consummate insiders, felt that everything, including the little children, belonged to them? Was it that Mr. Johnson saw a vulnerable child and felt that he could wrong her body, but leave his own soul and hers intact?

The abuse continued for more than two years; whenever Mr. Johnson could get her alone, he did. The last incident that Becca remembers was when she was about eight. She had actively avoided Mr. Johnson, counseling herself to stay away from him, to never let herself be alone with him. But on this day, for some reason, her vigilance was down. The family had been invited by people in the church to go horseback riding. They were in a barn, getting horses ready when suddenly Becca realized that she was alone with Mr. Johnson. Everyone had already left, and he was walking toward her. She remembers thinking, "How did I let this happen?" He picked her up and took her into a stall. "So appropriate," remembers Becca. "Among the horse shit."

What strikes Becca now is how absolutely typical her experience is. To be sexually abused in our society is no rarity. When you are a little girl with a single parent, your chances of being abused rise exponentially. Despite the suffering that abuse causes, there is nothing remarkable about it. Sexual abuse is so common, you can hardly walk into a room without confronting it.

Becca does not know why the abuse ended. Perhaps, she reasons, she just got too big for him to handle. When she was tiny, he could pick her up and carry her where he wanted her. Perhaps, it was that she learned words for what he was doing, and with words, power shifted. Regardless, he left her alone. As a child, she would sometimes lie in her bed at night and imagine concrete pouring down her throat, making her body heavy, until her consciousness could float above it and watch herself while the room grew long and distorted. Such a practice helped her sleep.

When she was fifteen, her sister told her that Mr. Johnson had had a heart attack. "I hate that man," she said to her sister. "You hate him, why?" her sister asked. It hadn't been until that moment that Becca recognized her hate. She hadn't really had memories of the abuse, except maybe some dreamlike ones. His daughters were frequently over at her house, and he was an unquestioned part of her milieu. With the acknowledgment of her hatred, memories of the abuse came back, but it would be a long time before she had the resources to deal with them.

Instead, Becca pushed herself to be good at everything. She loved church or at least churchliness. "I hated our own little church. I knew that it was pathetic," she says, but the greater church offered possibility. She loved the elements of the sacraments and the earthiness of the liturgical year. She loved the sense she had that her own church was a part of something much bigger. As much as Mr. Johnson had had power in her life, a more formidable force was her mother, who lived her faith with a passion for social justice and social transformation. Becca was elected the head of the Episcopal youth in the state of Tennessee. Her faith was something deeply personal. "I could always see the feeding of the five thousand," Becca says. "Myself there among the five thousand, and Jesus noticing me, caring about me, giving me a thumbs-up while he passed by. Does that sound silly?"

She excelled in school. She had an endless series of boyfriends, all of whom she was intimate with. "I don't know the psychology literature on abuse, but I do know that when your earliest, most intimate relationships with men are sexualized, that messes you up." She never had to learn the basics of sex. They were a part of her baseline reality constructed by Mr. Johnson. A way to be special.

She majored in math at Sewanee University in Tennessee, and then went to Washington, D.C., to work with Bread for the World. The first women were officially ordained in the Episcopal Church in the 1970s. But by 1985, when Becca was twenty-three, the ordination of women was starting to creep southward and the idea came into Becca's head to go to seminary. She returned to Nashville to attend Vanderbilt and pursue ordination in the Episcopal Church.

In Nashville, Becca met Marcus, the man who would become her husband. He was "cute and he played the guitar," but he was also "a healing presence for me, an utterly safe person." He was levelheaded and intellectual, a musician and philosopher. "Being in a relationship with someone who has been sexually abused is like being in a relationship with someone who has land mines all over her body. You never know what is going to set her off." It could be that Becca would have a bad session with the bishop and come home cursing all men and all people in authority everywhere. She might be in a relationship for a little while with someone and then decide out of the blue that he was really a predator who wanted to use her. She didn't want this to happen with Marcus, and since progress toward ordination required time with a therapist, Becca decided to look into the cause of her suffering.

Her memories of the abuse were dreamlike. They would bob to the surface and then disappear. In one of her books, she describes returning to the scene of the crime. The church had been sold and torn down. The sanctuary "deconsecrated." The site was now a Kroger parking lot. "It seemed right and holy and useful to build a place where people will actually be fed," she wrote. While she had been able to let go to a degree, she had not come far enough. In therapy she learned hypnosis. She told the therapist that hypnosis probably wouldn't work on her, since she was a very controlling person. But in fact, once she had the basics of hypnosis down, she realized that she had been practicing this for a long time. It had helped her preserve a sense of self. Self-hypnosis had been a survival technique learned from abuse. How to leave one's body was key.

Meanwhile, Becca finished seminary and was ordained two weeks before her first child, a boy, was born. She started working as chaplain at the university, and she frequently took students into the city to spend time with people who were hurting. To her, that was simply the bread and butter of the Christian life. In 2003, when the controversial question of the ordination of the Church's first openly gay bishop, Gene Robinson, was before the Episcopal Church, she testified about a dream she had had of her father. He had lifted up his hand to help her stand at the microphone in order to tell everyone not to worry. "Let Gene be a bishop and then get on with the work of the church, which is to clothe the naked and feed the hungry and love our enemies." Becca lived these words with her students. They spent time in homeless shelters, in Ecuador, in jails, and on the streets.

Along the way, another idea was percolating. The idea of sanctuary. Perhaps, she says, she was at first giving shape to the kind of sanctuary that she herself needed, but she also saw it as something that she could give to others. In her mind, the place was a beautiful space, a home, with a garden and flowering plants, spacious and full of light. "I pictured plants and beds and baskets of body products." It would be for women who were on the streets, who had been trapped and exploited, usually when they were too young to know any other life. Nearly immediately, she was able to articulate the ideals of the place: no one would have to pay one penny to be there, and they could stay for two full years. No figure of authority would live with them. Wherever this home was to be, even she would not have a key. It would belong to the people who lived in it. She knew only too well what figures of authority do to people who have been wounded by sexual abuse. She was determined to create a space where women felt absolutely safe. She imagined it to be a place where grace could do the work that it does: taking something that is wounded and turning it into something holy.

At the same time, she recognized that this vision was entirely her own. She didn't know if the same idea would resonate with women in jail. She decided that, before she built it, she'd better find out. Would they even be interested? She started conducting interviews with women in jail. These were women that our society has decided are so expendable that they don't even need resources for healing. When they run away from home as young girls, no one goes to look for them. There are no halfway houses for them, no rehabilitation programs aimed at them. No resources of any kind. When she started going to the jail and talking about the place she imagined, women wept. "When you say the word *home* in a jail, people start crying," Becca says diffidently.

The place came to be called Magdalene, and it has become a series of homes and a well-established program with now more than sixty graduates. But when Becca was starting it, something else was happening. Her son was turning five and heading to kindergarten. Becca fell apart. Her whole body became covered with hives. She had panic attacks. She found herself weeping uncontrollably. Five. Kindergarten. This was the age when everything collapsed. She realized that she needed to take another step toward healing. If she didn't, she would likely take out her pain on her children and on the women at Magdalene. She would convey even without meaning to that life was dangerous and frightening, that people couldn't be trusted. If she didn't heal, she wouldn't be a healing presence.

She was now a priest, active in the community, frequently asked to conduct weddings and funerals. At one such event, she encountered Mr. Johnson and his wife. There he was in the flesh. She struggled to conduct the wedding, her hands shaking. During the reception, Mr. Johnson and his wife approached Becca to tell her how proud they were of her, of what a wonderful priest she had become. She felt nauseous.

But the incident was instructive. Becca now knew what she needed to do. She needed to confront Mr. and Mrs. Johnson. She needed to hand back to them the burden that she had been carrying. Her husband and her mother offered to go with her, but she refused them. "The little girl who was abused by him was abused alone," she says. She wanted to honor that little girl by facing her abuser alone. She made an appointment with the Johnsons to come to their house and, to her surprise, they accepted. She decided to wear her priest's collar, a garment that, in reality, she hated. As a priest who frequently preaches barefoot, she hasn't worn it much before or since. Still it gave her the distance, the necessary authority, to say what she needed to say.

Sitting in the Johnson's living room, Becca said, "I need to tell you what happened to me a long time ago. I know it will be difficult for you to hear, but I have been carrying it a long time, and it is very heavy. I need to set it down, and you need to pick it up. I am going to tell this story. I am telling it without a lot of feeling. But if you want to know the feeling in it, it is compassion for myself when I was little. I was a wide-open, beautiful child, and that's the part of me you hurt."

As she started to speak, Mrs. Johnson grew pale and then physically ill. Becca continued calmly. "I'm sorry that what I am saying has made you sick, Mrs. Johnson. It has made me sick, too." She did feel, she says, compassion for them. She knew that she was ruining their lives, in a sense, but she also hoped that the truth might set them free.

Again to her surprise, Mr. Johnson denied nothing. His justifications for his actions were chilling: "I did it because you were so special to me. You were like a daughter." Then he asked, "Who have you told?"

"I thought, 'Oh, boy, you don't really want to ask me that question because the answer is—a lot of people.' "

Becca thought of Mr. Johnson's daughters and grand-daughters and shivered. She had no way of knowing how the history she was telling had affected them or how its implications would strike them. "I told him that I knew that I was a very open and loving little girl, and that that was the part of me that he abused. By the grace of God somehow he didn't take it from me. I told him that as much as I had suffered, an enormous amount of good had come from it. I got so many gifts out of it. I understand authority. I can walk into a room and feel who is safe and unsafe to me. Many other things."

Before she left, she asked them never to attend a funeral or a wedding that she was officiating. She told them that they had healing to work to do and she hoped that they would find help, but she wanted no part in it. She did not want reconciliation. She was not looking for closure with them. She did not want to see them again. And she never has. It is good for her, she says, that she let them go. She did not try to make nice or cover anything over.

Becca feels that the next stage is bringing this story to the church and telling it there. "We need to say to people that death and abuse do not have the last word. We need to acknowledge that abuse is not something that happens outside of the church, but frequently appears as a part of an ordinary religious child's growing up. We need to take a very hard look at this, and not imagine that we can change it with just a few seminars on child protection." She works to make herself and her office a safe place for people to tell their stories. "I invite them to tell not only the stories they have blamed themselves for, but the stories they don't even have words for."

"The story itself has hope, just in the telling," Becca says. Young people who come to her often say, "I just have to get over this," but Becca's experience is that a person doesn't really ever get over abuse or other forms of trauma. Healing often begins when a person begins to figure out how to incorporate the pain. "If somebody cuts off one of your legs when you are a kid, no matter how many times somebody says, 'Run, run,' you can't. You aren't made that way anymore. Abuse leaves a scar—physical evidence. A person says to herself, 'I am not right. I have nightmares or I can't eat or I gave someone a blow job and I didn't want to. I don't understand why that is.'

"While the scars do not go away, there is something deeper than the scars. That is the story I have to tell. What has been done for me is something that runs deeper than the scars can ever go. I feel the power to speak my truth in love without fear of retribution. I am not afraid to tell the truth. What can they do to you if you are not afraid?"

She now considers the ground where the abuse first took place—that old, moldy, clapboard house, a place long hated that has become a shopping mall—to be holy ground. "It was where my heart for women on the streets was born and where I took my first steps on a long and difficult path toward healing and forgiveness," she writes.

Conclusion: An Alternative Ethic

When I was twenty years old, a friend of mine was working on a photography project. As a women's studies major, she wanted to engage women in the process of creating photographs of themselves. The results would be a mixture of portrait and self-portrait. Marlene would be the photographer, but the subjects would be involved in the creation at every step. In principle, I thought this was a good idea. But collaboration with me proved difficult. I was an impossible subject. I loathed photographic images of myself, and I couldn't think of a single photo of me that I would want taken. After much conversation, we decided to do a photo session at the local coffee shop where she and I often went to write. When the proof sheet was ready, I looked at the photos with hatred. All of them were bad, I said. Not a single one did I want on display in the art building. We tried again along a creek bank where we sometimes walked. Again, I loathed the results and rejected them. Perhaps my dislike of the photographs was a form of youthful self-consciousness, akin to narcissism. But the fact was that I wanted out of this project, and I started thinking about how to tell Marlene.

Meanwhile, I was in the middle of significant changes. I was discarding the religiosity of my adolescence and trying to find something new. I was in and out of poor relationships with men, struggling to demand of them thoughtfulness and kindness. I found it harder than perhaps I should have to imagine myself as worthy of goodness. At root, I was trying to envision new and better ways of loving and being loved.

One day, Marlene and I were sitting in the lounge of our dormitory, discussing these things, when we struck on an idea. We decided to continue the photography project in the little chapel where I had been going for more than a year, alone, in an attempt to pray. Every morning, often before sunrise, I went to this little chapel for about an hour. It was an ongoing disastrous experiment that probably did the better part of killing my capacity for prayer for two decades. I spent the hour fighting sleep and chastising myself for dozing. I didn't know what prayer was, and attempting it on my own for such a long period of time meant that I was cultivating mostly self-disgust.

Marlene and I decided to take the camera to this chapel and photograph me naked. The idea was electrifying. We both felt startlingly alive as we contemplated it. But we were following the thought reflexively, without words for why. Perhaps I was seeking to put together the disparate parts of myself—the spiritual and the physical. I was in need of forging a union. I had a body that I did not know well, that seemed unreal to me, not an integrated part of myself.

This separation, which seemed like such a given, was unsatisfying and destructive. I was not good at being in the world. I didn't taste, touch, smell, hear, touch, or experience touch well. I didn't know the natural world at all. Distant from my physical being, my ability to experience the world was thin. I knew, instinctively, that I wanted more. This wanting led Marlene and me to Melby Chapel early on a gray February day, where we knew there was a lock on the door.

The chapel was empty and quiet when we arrived. We carefully locked the door. The chapel held a few pews, scattered copies of the Lutheran Book of Worship, and a few Bibles and hymnals. At the front were a pulpit, a table, and a three-paned stained-glass window. The light through the window was thin, and the chapel was cold. At first, I kept my clothes on.

As Marlene and I started photographing, I asked myself where I wanted to be. I curled up in front of the altar. I stood next to a plain cross on the wall. I stood in the crux of the stained-glass window. These were all places in the tiny chapel where I had never been. The surfaces and spaces were all new despite the fact that I had been coming there for a year. When I stepped out of my clothes and left them in a pile on the pew, I started to shake.

I went through the same series of photographs as before. I went to the altar and curled up. I stood next to the cross and in the stained glass window. Earlier in the project, Marlene had photographed our friend Diane, a pagan, naked in front of her potter's wheel. She was smeared with clay, utterly exalting in fleshiness. Being a naked Christian seemed harder, to say the least. I felt I had to extract my body from the narrowest margins of my life. I had to force into juxtaposition a cross and my own body.

My skin prickled with sensation. The cement floor pressed into my knees. My hands grew cold touching the wall. Nothing I touched had any softness in it. The cross and I stayed apart as if magnetically repelled. Yet for all the coldness of the room and for all its lack of welcome for my naked self, I could now feel profoundly a yearning that I hadn't known was there—a yearning for warmth, for vulnerability, for the chapel to see me naked, to see that I dared, for once, to bring my whole self to church.

This time, when the proof sheets came back, energy

and electricity pulsed through them. I felt that I had struck upon a new power, something I was just beginning to perceive, but that I sensed would reverberate. What I had struck upon was a possibility buried deep in Christianity itself. The Gospel, writes Gerard Loughlin, "has always been a story of carnal desire and erotic encounter." God longs for flesh, for humanity, longs for the connection and, so, for the sake of love and desire, takes on flesh.

In many of the stories in this book, we can see the stirrings of practices that take on this same challenge. For Matthew, it is the stillness of allowing his pain to be present in a form that is close to contemplative prayer. For Ashley, it is the embodiment of liturgy. For Paul, it is the enfleshed word found in preaching. For Genevieve and Becca, it is the transformation of deep wounds into good work. For me, it is the routinized practice of the soup kitchen, where strangers meet and share hospitality. None of these forms are new to Christianity. All of them have ancient roots. Yet each, I would argue, has an erotic element—a way that body and spirit meet in a way that is life-giving and energizing, that gives and receives love.

Finding eroticism at the soup kitchen is a tough thing for me to admit. I know that I am supposed to be doing charity work, helping others, practicing being good. But the soup kitchen isn't really any of these things for me. It is the practice of allowing my body and spirit to be energized with the presence of others, of learning to let love flow through my hands.

Erotic energy can, no doubt, be dangerous energy. We've seen many times the damage that it, when improperly used, does to people and communities. But shutting it out is not the answer. Instead we need to find practices to embody more fully this life-giving energy, its potential to transform and to heal.

Whenever I contemplate this, I think of a man I'll call Jim. He was a fixture at the Community Meal where I work every Tuesday. He was the most sexually damaged person I have ever encountered. His relationships with his family had been severed over accusations of sexual misconduct with children, accusations I don't doubt. He lived alone in a grimy apartment, where, others reported to me, he spent a lot of time smoking pot and watching pornographic videos. At the soup kitchen, he was frequently loud and inappropriate. He was in love with another soup kitchen cook, and he often made sexual innuendos to and about her. He stood in the door of the kitchen watching me work. "Jim, how are you?" I said. His answer was invariably a chuckle and "No damn good." At that point, I usually suggested he have a seat in the dining room and a cup of coffee.

One year, as a part of Holy Week, the church held a foot-washing service, and strangely enough, only four of us, including Jim, showed up. We set up an intimate circle in the sanctuary with basins of warm water and fresh towels. We read the story of Jesus washing the feet of his disciples and then we began to wash one another's feet. When it was Jim's turn to have his feet washed, he started to shake, almost uncontrollably, but he did not run away. He stayed rooted to his chair while our female priest bent and gently washed his feet. I cannot quite find words for what it was like to watch a person stripped of all pretense, having his vulnerable self revealed by the simple act of touch. He was trembling. If we'd had a blanket in the church, and I wish we had, I would have covered him. The priest washed his feet carefully. She did not rush. When she was finished, she dried his feet with a towel. Then it was his turn. He bent and washed my feet, as gently, as carefully as his had been washed.

I won't claim that a radical transformation happened that night. It's true that I never again heard a sexual innuendo from Jim directed at me or the other cook, but he still said inappropriate things. He was still frequently loud and annoying, lonely and sad. Toward the end of his life, he grew angrier and more scared, and we struggled to be with him in the ways that he needed. But I do think that healing power existed in those few moments that we spent washing feet. If healing and wholeness is an ongoing work, if repairing the world, as the Jewish tradition says, comes from our alignment with the loving and erotic work of God, then I would say that we joined with it that night—all four of us. We touched it, if only briefly.

Perhaps because I have wanted to talk about sexuality and spirituality in new ways, I have been reluctant to offer, as a result of these stories, a sexual ethic. I have not wanted to answer the question, "What is it right to do?" But as I have studied what people told me, I have defined some principles that I think can guide us toward a more complete and holy understanding of sexuality than the conflicted one we have now that take so many on a path of fear and alienation. These are not new rules. They are instead mechanisms for listening to the stories of others and to our own stories.

People often encounter stories about the relationship between spirituality and sexuality through a lens of judgment. They want to know whether a particular action is right or wrong. They use these rules to inflict pain on themselves and on other people. In place of judgment, I would offer the value of discernment. Discernment, Nora Gallagher writes, is the power to grow quiet and listen deeply. Discernment means that we do not place ourselves in a position to judge other people's stories, pleasures, or realities. We do not prescribe behavior for each other. Because we have not prejudged situations and people, we expand our capacity to see and to know them for what they are. Knowing that sexuality is a source for a great deal of pain and hurt, we are able to discern what behavior is truly damaging to ourselves and to others, and we are also able to discern what intervention is appropriate and possible. We can also discern when sexuality that might "break the rules" is a source of joy and of hope. Because nonjudgment means that we no longer look to an external list of rules to tell us what is "right" and "wrong," it also means that we have to hone our powers of discernment. This principle is threatening to those terrified of the very freedom to which our religious tradition calls us, but it is essential if we are to find an alternative to our current state of alienation between the body and spirit.

The second principle is the cultivation of wonder instead of fear. Many of the people I interviewed for this book grew up with the idea that, if they made one mistake, they would fall into doom and misery. Sexual mistakes had the most dire consequences. Thus, sexuality became ensconced in fear—fear of being found out, fear of truly being known, fear of failing. Yet, nearly everyone I interviewed had found a way through fear and found their deepest intimacy with God in their capacity for wonder.

In the fourteenth century, in the midst of a church torn apart by rampant disease, violent power struggles, and burnings of heretics, Julian of Norwich, the first woman to write a book in English, wrote these lines: "The soul must perform two duties. The first is to always wonder and be surprised. The second is to endure, always taking pleasure in God." I take Julian to be playing with the word *duty* here, reversing our expectations for what our "duties" are. Instead of placing a still heavier burden on the soul, she suggests that we are called to a state of wonder and delight. She coaxes us out of jaded certainty into a place where we can truly be surprised by ourselves, other people, and the multifaceted, complex, and ever-changing world around us.

I tie wonder to an alternative sexual ethic because we are called out of what we already "know" about sexuality to what might yet surprise and transform us. We anticipate delight that turns a world of rules on its head. We approach our own sexuality with the potential for the unexpected— what is it I have yet to know about myself? How can I love better? Wonder suggests that our sexuality is not a finished state, but a way that we can still be taught, reached, and pursued by the Holy. Julian hints that the process of discovery may even be infinite as she asks that we "always" wonder and be surprised. Wonder eats away at fear because it teaches that the surprises that await may be just as delightful as they may be painful. We desire to know more and to fear less.

Wonder turns us toward the cultivation of aliveness in ourselves and in others. As we grow in discernment and wonder, we also cultivate our senses and our engagement with the sensual world. A great deal of the world around us, abetted by our individual histories, compels us to numbness, to sensory deprivation. We do not spend time in nature; we live in cocoons that rarely subject us to the realities of hot and cold; we eat bland food as quickly as possible so that we can get on with our work, usually in a sensory-deprived environment like our cars or an office. By living in this deficient atmosphere, we do damage to our sexuality and our spirituality at the same time, at the very point where they are connected: our senses.

In this alternative sexual ethic, we commit to addressing whatever part of us that seeks to be numb and dead instead of an active and living presence in the world. This principle asks us to rigorously address whatever it is that keeps us from living and being fully present to ourselves and to each other. This includes attention to the sensory world—taste, smell, touch, sight, and sound—and attention to all that is available for us to be awake to, including both the natural and humanly constructed worlds. Aliveness is a process and not a destination, so we must respond with compassion to ourselves and each other as we encounter blindness and numbness, when our old habits sneak up on us and change into evermore compelling illusions.

Aliveness is essential to our sexuality because, through it, we allow ourselves to feel both pain and pleasure, and we grow in connectedness to other people. Attentiveness is fundamental to loving ourselves, our neighbor, and God. It has to be cultivated and practiced. It involves trial and error. Aliveness does not mean that we feel good at every moment. It does mean that we seek to understand and accept pain as it comes—often in ways and for reasons that we do not understand. As we move into aliveness and attentiveness, we of necessity move away from the realm of rules. We have to be present to what *is* in the moment and give up some of our expectation for what an external standard says there *should* be. I am not advocating absolute relativism as some would imagine, because through attentiveness, we are able to discern what is right and wrong, but we are less able to proclaim that our discoveries hold for every person who ever lived throughout all history and geography. As aliveness works together with discernment, we begin to find our own very defined path.

True, deep, real pleasure is an avenue to the Holy. Through discernment, wonder, and aliveness, we will know what real pleasure is. We will be able to determine—actively, bodily, and through our senses—what Julian means by "taking pleasure in God." And when we sense true pleasure, we will trust it and be able to act boldly in it and with it.

Pleasure is, perhaps, on the surface the most dangerous of my suggestions. We associate pleasure with narcissism, with excess, hedonism, and self-indulgence. The kind of pleasure I am speaking of, however, is actually quite in opposition. If we pay very close attention, I think we will find that the pleasures of excess, hedonism, and self-indulgence are thin. Deeper, wider, more lasting pleasures are available as we grow more attentive to and more comfortable in our own skins, and as we give up the notion that pleasure is inherently selfish. The deepest pleasures that I know—and certainly I don't have the definitive word—are fairly simple and involve connectedness to other people. Cooking at the soup kitchen is one for me. This is not an act of "duty" or "responsibility." It's an act of real, sensual pleasure. So is a good long hike and a hot bath after it, a cross-country ski at dawn when I watch the sun begin to cast light on the western mountains, an evening making love with my husband, a note of delight in my son's voice. We're not talking about what Sarah Coakley calls being "carelessly happy or unhappily careless." We are talking about the way that God speaks to us through real pleasure and about learning what real pleasure is so that we can listen.

These principles guide us toward a different way of being spiritual and sexual at the same time. It opens up a variety of possibilities that might have been closed in a rule-governed ethic. Using this ethic, we might, for example, teach our children differently, asking them first for a deep self-respect and self-knowledge before we impose a set of absolute rules for them to follow. A close friend has a daughter just entering puberty. This eleven-year-old is very reluctant about adulthood. She would prefer, she has told her mother, to stay in childhood, and she cannot imagine what the path ahead holds for her that she might like. One of her mother's answers surprised me. It was an answer that my own mother could never have offered me. She told her daughter, "Your body will know more pleasure than you can even now imagine. You are going through a period where your body is going to learn to feel pleasure, and you will be amazed." In a sense, she gave her daughter pleasure as a guide to growing up. She asked her to pay attention, to herself, to others, in order to understand what maturity looks like. We all know that puberty, adolescence, adulthood are not solely about pleasure. A greater capacity for pain also comes with the greater capacity for pleasure that her mother pointed to. But pain we know well. Pleasure we sometimes need help attending to.

We also might learn to encounter our sexuality in sacred settings without fear. If we remain honest with ourselves and with each other, if we root and ground ourselves in love, the truth of our sexual existence might take us to places that are unexpected. Christianity is a pretty strange religion when you look closely at it. At the center of Christianity is a ritual where we eat the body and drink the blood of someone else. However symbolic you want to make it, we accept eating someone's body and drinking blood as a link between the ordinary and the extraordinary, between the natural and the supernatural.

When I take communion, I am enacting a mysterious intimacy with Christ, a relationship so close that I take Christ's body into my own, and it becomes a part of me. I do this in community with others who are also known as "the Body of Christ." At the center of my faith is a ritual that asks me for sensual intimacy not only with Christ, but also with others. Even if I find it more comfortable to deny that there are also sexual elements present in this central ritual, "bodies," both symbolic and actual, both ordinary and extraordinary, both my own and God's, are foundational to the Christian faith. We are asked to take God into our mouths. To me, that's a pretty powerful mystery. Some of its power comes from the radical, sensual presence of God that asks us to be alive to ourselves and to each other through the very tangible means of bread and wine.

If nothing else, these stories about very ordinary people's ordinary struggles to live as whole beings in our very particular culture, teach us, I hope, respect for telling our stories. As Becca says, "The story itself has hope, just in the telling." Perhaps we can learn to grant to one another, in the Body of Christ, an opportunity to speak truth in love and to forge ahead toward wholeness.

Acknowledgments

Thanks especially to the people who generously offered their stories to this book, who read drafts, offered feedback, and worked to get the stories as right as they could be. My admiration for each of you is deep.

To Lil Copan and Kathy Helmers for their help and thoughtfulness in developing the concept of this book.

To Amy Caldwell for lively conversations and for seeing it through.

To Bill Frank at the Colorado Mountain College library for ordering books like *Solitary Sex: A Cultural History of Masturbation* without blinking.

To Peter Boumgarden for sharing his bibliographic mind.

To the women of Magdalene for their astonishing insight.

To Peter Frykholm, body, mind, and spirit.

To Sam.

To the women of the Writers' Bloc. This book began one day around the table with all of you writing a meditation on the hands of Abraham Lincoln.

To Ali Lufkin. This book would not exist without all that I learned from you.

Resources

Au, Wilkie, SJ. *By Way of the Heart: Toward a Holistic Christian Spirituality.* Mahwah, NJ: Paulist Press, 1989.

Bordo, Susan. *Unbearable Weight: Feminism, Western Culture, and the Body.* Berkeley: University of California Press, 1993.

Boyd, Malcolm. *Half Laughing, Half Crying: Songs for Myself.* New York: St. Martin's Press, 1986.

Brown, Peter. *The Body and Society: Men, Women and Sexual Renunciation in Early Christianity.* New York: Columbia University Press, 1988.

Browning, Don, M. Christian Green, and John Witte Jr., eds. *Sex, Marriage, and Family in World Religions.* New York: Columbia University Press, 2006.

Coakley, Sarah, ed. *The New Asceticism.* New York: Continuum, 2011.

———. *Religion and the Body.* Cambridge: Cambridge University Press, 1997.

Coogan, Michael. *God and Sex: What the Bible Really Says.* New York: Grand Central Publishing, 2010.

Davies, Jon, and Gerard Loughlin. *Sex These Days: Essays on Theology, Sexuality and Society.* London: Sheffield, 1997.

Davis, Erik. *Techgnosis: Myth, Magic and Mysticism in the Age of Information.* New York: Harmony Books, 1998.

Ellison, Marvin M., and Sylvia Thorson-Smith, eds. *Body and Soul: Rethinking Sexuality as Justice-Love*. Cleveland: Pilgrim Press, 2003.

Farley, Margaret. *Just Love: A Framework for Christian Sexual Ethics*. New York: Continuum, 2006.

Gallagher, Nora. *Practicing Resurrection: A Memoir of Work, Doubt, Discernment, and Moments of Grace*. New York: Knopf, 2003.

Glaser, Chris. *Come Home! Reclaiming Spirituality and Community as Gay Men and Lesbians*. San Francisco: Harper and Row, 1990.

Hawkes, Gail. *Sex and Pleasure in Western Culture*. Cambridge: Polity Press, 2004.

Ind, Jo. *Memories of Bliss: God, Sex, and Us*. London: SCM Press, 2003.

Jones, Beth Felker. *Marks of His Wound: Gender Politics and Body Determinism*. New York: Oxford University Press, 2007.

Jordan, Mark D. *Blessing Same-Sex Unions: The Perils of Queer Romance and the Confusions of Christian Marriage*. Chicago: University of Chicago Press, 2005.

———. *Telling Truths in Church: Scandal, Flesh, and Christian Speech*. Boston: Beacon Press, 2003.

Julian of Norwich. *The Writings of Julian of Norwich: A Vision Showed to a Devout Woman* and *A Revelation of Divine Love*. Nicholas Watson and Jacqueline Jenkins, eds. University Park, PA: Pennsylvania State University Press, 2006.

Laqueur, Thomas. *Making Sex: Body and Gender from the Greeks to Freud*. Cambridge, MA: Harvard University Press, 1990.

———. *Solitary Sex: A Cultural History of Masturbation*. Zone Books, 2003.

Loader, William. *Sexuality in the New Testament: Understanding the Key Texts.* Louisville, KY: Westminster John Knox Press, 2010.

Loughlin, Gerard. *Alien Sex: The Body and Desire in Cinema and Theology.* London: Blackwell, 2004.

Mairs, Nancy. *Remembering the Bone House: The Erotics of Place and Space.* Boston: Beacon Press, 1995.

Marion, Jean-Luc. *The Erotic Phenomenon.* Chicago: University of Chicago Press, 2007.

Miles, Margaret. *Carnal Knowing: Female Nakedness and Religious Meaning in the Christian West.* New York: Vintage Books, 1989.

———. *Practicing Christianity: Critical Perspectives for an Embodied Spirituality.* Eugene, OR: Wipf and Stock, 2006.

———. *Word Made Flesh: A History of Christian Thought.* Oxford, UK: Blackwell, 2005.

Miles, Sara. *Take This Bread: A Radical Conversion.* New York: Ballantine Books, 2007.

Nelson, James, and Sandra P. Longfellow, eds. *Sexuality and the Sacred: Sources for Theological Reflection.* Louisville, KY: Westminster John Knox Press, 1994.

Niebuhr, Reinhold. *The Nature and Destiny of Man: A Christian Interpretation.* Louisville, KY: Westminster John Knox Press, 1996.

Sherrard, Philip. *Christianity: Lineaments of a Sacred Tradition.* Edinburgh: T&T Clark, 1998.

Silverman, Sue. *Love Sick: One Woman's Journey through Sexual Addiction.* New York: W. W. Norton, 2001.

Stevens, Becca. *Hither and Yon: A Travel Guide for the Spiritual Journey.* Nashville, TN: Abingdon Press, 2007.

———. *Sanctuary: Unexpected Places Where God Found Me.* Nashville, TN: Abingdon Press, 2005.

Talbot, Alice-Mary, ed. "St. Mary of Egypt." In Alice-Mary Talbot, ed., *Holy Women of Byzantium: 10 Saints' Lives in English Translation*. Washington, D.C.: Dumbarton Oaks Research Library and Collection, 2006.

Teilhard de Chardin, Pierre. *The Heart of Matter*. New York: Harcourt Brace Jovanovich, 1978.

Tine, Moussa. From "A Saint in the City: Sufi Arts of Northern Senegal." Exhibition text. Santa Fe, NM: Museum of International Folk Art, 2007.

Williams, Rowan. "The Body's Grace." In Eugene F. Rogers Jr., ed., *Theology and Sexuality: Classic and Contemporary Readings*. London: Blackwell, 2002.